Covenant and
Community
in Modern
Judaism

Recent Titles in
Contributions to the Study of Religion

Covenant and Community in Modern Judaism

S. Daniel Breslauer

CONTRIBUTIONS TO THE STUDY OF RELIGION, NUMBER 21
Henry Warner Bowden, Series Editor

GREENWOOD PRESS
New York • Westport, Connecticut • London

BM
612.5
.B74
1989

Library of Congress Cataloging-in-Publication Data

Breslauer, S. Daniel.
    Covenant and community in modern Judaism / S. Daniel Breslauer.
        p. cm . — (Contributions to the study of religion, ISSN
0196-7053; no. 21)
    Bibliography: p.
    Includes index.
    ISBN 0-313-26605-0 (lib. bdg. : alk. paper)
    1. Covenants (Jewish theology) — History of doctrines. 2. Judaism —
History — Modern period, 1750- I. Title. II. Series.
BM612.5.B74 1989
296.3'11 — dc19   88-24631

British Library Cataloguing in Publication Data is available.

Library of Congress Catalog Card Number: 88-24631
ISBN: 0-313-26605-0
ISSN: 0196-7053

First published in 1989

Greenwood Press, Inc.
88 Post Road West, Westport, Connecticut 06881

Printed in the United States of America

The paper used in this book complies with the Permanent Paper Standard
issued by the National Information Standards Organization (Z39.48-1984).

10 9 8 7 6 5 4 3 2 1

Contents

Foreword

Since the Diaspora it has been quite a challenge to discuss Judaism generically, to capture varying phenomena within an adequately representative set of characteristics. Some think it almost as difficult to treat Judaism uniformly in earlier periods, before the homeland was lost. After both of those epochs various cultures in medieval and modern times have affected this ancient religious tradition in many ways. The textures and voices, emphases and values, in present-day Jewish groups are so diverse that some might wonder if any common denominator can suffice to unite all the different expressions of contemporary Judaism. In face of Hasidism, Orthodoxy, Reform, Reconstructionism, and even "checkbook Judaism," what can undergird all of these structures?

The brief overview provided here by Professor S. Daniel Breslauer makes a bold effort to place contemporary Judaism on one such constant. Nothing is comprehensive enough to include all aspects of different Jewish communities, but the concept of covenant is serviceable in discussing Jewish history as well as its multiple expressions. Covenantal relationships go back as far as the time of Moses and, from that perspective, make the concept applicable to Abraham and events prior to tribal consolidation. The idea of a special compact between Yahweh and Israel as a chosen people has been flexible enough to accommodate many circumstantial changes. Kingdom, exile from and restoration to the land around Jerusalem, lasting dispersion after 70 C.E., settlement throughout Europe, pogroms, Zionism, and now a resuscitated state of Israel—all these have been settings in which the covenant proved useful in interpreting experience and exhorting the faithful to acknowledge their unique responsibilities.

So Professor Breslauer chooses wisely when he utilizes this malleable yet tenacious concept as a perennial Jewish theme. Part of its fascination is the different forms it takes and the widely varying circumstances in which it can supply meaningful guidance. Another remarkable aspect is the way it serves to knit otherwise dissimilar groups together, providing cohesiveness to a rich accumulation of rituals and piety. Judaism has experienced much, and expressions of its many insights have taken a variety of forms. Judaism has survived much, and its different voices help us appreciate the continuity that undergirds multiple changes. Its life-styles and ideologies are many; its vitality is undisputed. Covenantal thought lies at the heart of such continuous strength. This thoughtful reflection on covenant as a fundamental component in Judaism presents readers with an opportunity to make their own inquiry into an ancient and resilient faith. It offers not an exhaustive analysis but rather an invitation to consider what links contemporary religion with tradition and what gives it a capacity to meet tomorrow's challenges.

Henry Bowden

Preface

In January 1987, I spent a month in Jerusalem as part of a theological seminar discussing the idea of covenant and election. The meeting was sponsored by the National Council of Christians and Jews, under the direction of Paul Van Buren. The opportunity included discussions with David Hartman and study at the Hartman Institute in Jerusalem, an invaluable resource. The interchange with an international group of cordial and demanding colleagues proved to be the most exciting part of the seminar for me. I left the seminar convinced that the concept of covenant represented the most central theological idea for contemporary Judaism.

This book distills a variety of studies and reflections on modern Judaism. Contemporary theologians have focused on covenant as a biblical category applicable to modern religion. This focus proves to be of significant importance in light of the challenges modernity raises for any traditional religion. Judaism, in particular, has encountered problems both when Jews adapt to modern life and when they reject it. Utilizing the covenant concept as a means of revitalizing contemporary Judaism, however, involves problems of its own. While scholars agree on the centrality of the concept in biblical religion, they often disagree in their evaluations of its meaning and significance, particularly for contemporary Jews. A new definition of covenant is needed to bring order to this scholarly chaos.

The argument offered here takes account of the biblical data, the debates among scholars, and the theological interpretations often given as explanations or excuses for covenantal religion. A number of common themes — the problems of being a Jew in the modern world, comprehending human freedom, dialogue with others — and common thinkers — predominantly Jacob Agus, Martin Buber, Maurice Friedman, David Hartman, Will Herberg, and Abraham Joshua Heschel — and common sources — Hasidism generally and Rabbi Menahem Mendel of Kotzk in particular, stories about talmudic rabbis, the Hebrew Bible — link every chapter in the book. These references, however, do not suggest that this book offers a definitive analysis of any of these. Each is taken seriously as a stepping stone on a quest across shifting waters. The main purpose of the quest, however, is creative — to suggest ways in which covenantal images offer realistic and potentially positive answers to the problems posed by modern society for contemporary Jews.

The study begins with an introduction that establishes the basic elements in "covenantal Judaism." The second chapter explores the problems raised by that covenantal paradigm, particularly as articulated by theologian Richard Rubenstein. The next three chapters explore the possibilities for a positive covenantal religion in response to that critique. The conclusion draws the various themes together in a proposal for covenantal theology as a basis of affirming Jewish religion as a valid modern option.

Support for the research in this study has been given through grant number 3722–xx–0038 of the General Research Fund of the University of Kansas. I gratefully acknowledge that help. I have shared the progress of this work in tentative form with colleagues too numerous to mention, both as papers at professional meetings and as articles, unrecognizable in the shape they have finally taken. I thank my colleagues for their criticism, advice, and support.

My wife, Fran, and my children, Don and Tamar, have been

supportive and helpful during my work on this project. Whatever a person does reflects more than academic influences, and for me the influence of my family cannot be calculated.

My aim in writing this book is to stimulate careful thinking and sensitive self-reflection. Whether I succeed in that attempt or not, readers alone can judge. My central hope is that readers will find the ideas expressed stimulating enough to begin a dialogue of their own and discover how their own identities and concerns may be nurtured by a religious tradition.

Covenant and
Community
in Modern
Judaism

1

Introduction: The Meaning of Covenant

DEFINING COVENANT IN JUDAISM

Many contemporary theologians, both Jewish and non-Jewish, characterize biblical thinking, and, by extension, Jewish thinking as "covenantal."[1] The meaning of such a designation, however, hardly seems clear. Some scholars suggest that the biblical covenant may have drawn on ancient Near Eastern treaty forms; other scholars note the variety of covenant types in the Hebrew Bible — covenants between human beings, between human beings and God, covenants with individuals, covenants with communities, unilateral covenants, stipulative covenants, unconditional covenants. Even those theologians who take covenant as their central metaphor for Jewish religion rarely give a precise definition. In this way, for example, David Hartman argues for a "covenantal anthropology" based on his understanding of God's interaction with the Jewish people at Mount Sinai. In developing his argument, however, Hartman draws on covenants with Noah and Abraham, explicitly rejecting the covenant with David as normative. His approach results in a careful analysis of contemporary Jewish predicaments, but it does not clarify the meaning or significance of the concept "covenant" in an unambiguous way. This method of generating an independent model and then grouping various biblical illustrations around it may prove a helpful means of revitalizing Judaism today. Hartman's suggestion that covenant represents a combination of human audacity and realization of divine power provides a powerful critique of both liberal and traditionalist approaches to Judaism. When, however, this method proceeds without a careful definition of the concept providing the basic paradigm, it holds the potential for misuse.[2]

Rabbi Hayim Halevy Donin's energetic defense of Judaism, *To Be a Jew*, illustrates the problems inherent in such a method.[3] Donin's purpose seems to be to revitalize Jewish practice by presenting the teachings of *halakha*, Jewish law, within a persuasive theological setting. The idea of covenant offers him a theological means of justifying legal ordinances and of rationalizing Israel's "election" and the description of God as "the God of Israel" (thus he explains that such a locution "is only to remind ourselves of our covenant with the universal God to whom all mankind owes allegiance"). When he actually describes covenantal actions, however, he neglects to provide a consistent interpretation that would link them with his theory. In discussing circumcision, "the covenant of Abraham," for example, he offers no justification for calling such an act covenantal nor an indication of how such a rite might be a reminder of the universal God. A consistent view of covenant needs to apply a more precise definition to specific cases of Jewish action and ritual performances.

Covenant, as just noted, does not lend itself to any unambivalent definition. Both the Hebrew word for covenant, *ber'it*, and the concept it implies are used with various meanings throughout the Hebrew Bible and Jewish tradition. Perhaps the very process of definition needs to be reviewed. Richard Robinson surveys the problems and debates surrounding attempts to discover definitions. He traces various theories about "meaning" and "defining," concluding that "words are primarily a means by which *humans* deal with *things*." He then suggests three ways in which words can be connected with their objects:

a real definition identifies the thing with the word describing it; a lexical definition records what things a word customarily describes; a stipulative definition seeks "the removal of an ambiguity and the avoidance of an inconvenience caused by the ambiguity."[4] In practice this last way proves the most useful. It acknowledges the limits of all uses of language and the inherent ambiguity in words and restricts its claims to those of a specifically delineated task. The lexical definition summarizes usage but rarely moves beyond the confusion and ambiguity inherent in almost every word. The real definition assumes an essence that exists independently of human language. In fact, however, "there is no such thing as essence in the sense intended," since all language merely reflects human choice. The search for an essence ignores the lack of inherent connection between a word chosen and the external reality to which it refers. Stipulative definitions promise to become points of departure for ongoing investigation and discussion; they become occasions for human study rather than conclusions of such study.[5]

Covenant as a theological idea needs such a stipulative definition because of the variety of meanings and uses for which it has been employed. Even the biblical data present a bewildering picture of diverse and often conflicting views of covenant. One scholar, Dennis McCarthy, notes that not only do different biblical texts understand the concept differently, the different meanings do not seem to "evolve" in any progressive or definable way. He comments that "it is impossible to bring all the interpretations of the various covenants together under one definition or a simple linear line of development."[6] For the sake of this study, then, a review of the biblical material elucidates one set of covenantal ideas, not its "true" meaning.

The stipulative definition provided here utilizes basic themes found throughout the biblical tradition. Covenant, defined according to this stipulative definition, entails two constitutive properties: it consists of a set of obligations and expectations and a relationship between the deity and human beings. The ambiguity of covenant—applying to either an agreement made by an individual or by a community as a whole with the deity—suggests its multifaceted nature. Biblical covenants often involve individual responsibility. Individuals expect God to act towards them in a special way, and they recognize special obligations towards the deity. Other covenants are more communal. Each of these cases, however, exemplifies one basic reality—God and humanity share a common ground. God enters into human life and allows human beings to affect history. On the basis of this analysis any covenant must include a set of expectations and obligations that create a common sphere of activity between the divine and the human. Biblical covenant in general, then, represents an agreement, a contract, a "pact," between a divine being and humanity. The deity gives promises to human beings and exacts promises from them; human beings expect the deity to respond in certain ways to their actions. In the case of the Jewish people the deity exclusively chooses one human being or one human community; that human being or community devotes exclusive loyalty to the deity. Covenant as used in the Bible, therefore, illustrates, "a pact between a deity and a people . . . the only one to demand exclusive loyalty and preclude the possibility of dual or multiple loyalties."[7]

The meaning of covenant as stipulated here consists of one set of formal constituents and one theological assertion. Covenant religion provides obligations for its followers and promises them expectations for both fulfillment and neglect of those obligations. Secondly, it defines that set of obligations and expectations in terms of God. By performing such actions, individuals enter "the common ground of man and God."[8] Studying covenant means studying the specific types of obligations in any particular pact, the expectations that reinforce those obligations, and the theology supporting the claims that this pact creates a shared sphere of activity for the divine and the human.

The Hebrew Bible records such contractual covenants throughout its three sections, the Torah, the Prophets, and the

Writings, each of which needs explication. While the structure presented here takes an evolutionary or progressive shape, that form represents a theological imposition. The tripartite division of the Hebrew Bible is used as a convenient organizational principle and should not be taken as the source of the divisions discussed. Nevertheless, this order of development sets the basic pattern for the rest of this study and reappears as a major theme in subsequent chapters.

COVENANT IN THE TORAH

The Torah emphasizes Israel's covenant with God. The Book of Genesis introduces the idea of God's will as the basis for stability and order despite the human inclination to evil. Genesis 8–9 describe how, after God has destroyed the world by flood, God proclaims the human inclination evil from youth. In consequence, God establishes a covenant whereby humanity enjoys certain rights and must fulfill certain obligations. This covenant with the survivor of the flood, in later Jewish thinking, emphasizes basic human responsibilities.

The biblical narrative itself augments the covenant with Noah by a series of covenants with Israel's early ancestors — Abraham, Isaac, and Jacob. The nature of these covenants is often extremely individualized and personal. Thus Abraham finds assurance that his descendants will become a great nation (Genesis 17) and in exchange discovers the obligation to perform circumcision; Jacob (Genesis 28) agrees to tithe his wealth in exchange for divine protection.

The most extensive treatment of covenantal obligation, however, occurs in the stories and laws associated with Israel's Exodus from Egypt. According to the tradition, when God rescued the Israelites from Egyptian slavery, they responded by agreeing to obey divine commandments. Exodus 19–20 relates the events of this covenant-making. The Israelites, brought before God, listen to a list of stipulations, some of them cultic, some ethical, and some civil, and accept them.

They gain from this a national identity and they become a "holy" people, while each individual gains an identity. Throughout the Torah the personal identity established by obedience to the obligations of the covenant is as important as the communal one: covenant leads to the expectation of meaning in personal life. This may be rendered in more modern language as "selfhood." To become a self means to establish a set of priorities, to accept one's own talents and limitations, and to recognize both one's potential for the future and one's debt to the past. Covenant agreement in the Torah enables every Jew to achieve such a sense of self.

The central idea here — covenant provides a sense of self through its combination of social and personal obligations — derives from a general institution in the ancient Near East, the treaty binding one nation to another. This formal declaration follows certain established patterns: it includes a review of history, a statement of relationship, a list of detailed obligations and expectations for both parties to the treaty, provisions for publicizing the treaty, and concluding stipulations and sanctions in case the treaty is broken. This structure, reproduced with varying degrees of detail in the Torah, became the basis for Israelite self-understanding. Covenant, understood in this way, focuses on those obligations that Jews must follow as a consequence of their identity, of whom they are. The Torah offers various covenantal statements that reflect this formal order (see Exodus 19–23, 33–34; Leviticus 18–23; Deuteronomy 12–27). These laws form the most explicit teaching of the Torah.

Many scholars find traces of the covenant form throughout the Torah. Gerhard von Rad has analyzed Deuteronomy 26, for example, and discovered that it preserves a miniature covenant, an early "credo" recited by the Israelites.[9] The actual stipulations enumerated in Deuteronomy 26 and the specific expectations that range from personal prosperity through national security evolved over a long period of time. The actual "confession" of faith, however, the historical recitation itself, may very well be ancient. The historical background given for covenantal religion in the passage is characteristically related to a dramatic event purported to have occurred at the beginning of Israel's history:

> A wandering Aramean was my father who migrated into Egypt, living there few in number, and there he became a great, mighty, and populous nation. But the Egyptians treated us harshly by afflicting us and enslaving us. Then we petitioned the Lord, the God of our ancestors, and the Lord attended to our petition, noting our affliction, toil, and suffering, so that the Lord brought us out of Egypt with a mighty hand and an outstretched arm. (Deuteronomy 26:5–8)

This historical review is more important for its implication about Israelite obligations than for its accuracy. It emphasizes that the Israelites are dependent upon God for their national consciousness (God transformed the Aramean father into a new nation) and for their independence (God brought them from slavery into freedom) and that therefore the Israelites are required to perform certain religious rituals (primarily petitioning the Lord). This confession of history occurs in the midst of a series of commandments concerning treatment of strangers, ritual purity, and religious authorities. Covenant identity, rooted in historical memory, entails specific personal obligations.

David Novak comments on the ambivalent ways Jewish tradition expresses this idea. At times it emphasizes the Jewish decision to obey the divine commandments. On the other hand, some rabbinic commentators explain that the Jews were coerced into accepting the Torah, that they had no choice but could only accede to a power greater than themselves.[10] Both views suggest actual concerns animating the Torah story. At times people freely affirm their identity, they choose the groups with which they associate, they determine the culture they will follow. At other times, however, people find their identity thrust upon them, they cannot escape the historical forces that have molded and shaped them. Will Herberg echoes this sense of inevitability when he denies that covenant is "a private act of agreement and affiliation" and says that it is, rather, "an objective supernatural fact."[11] One form of covenantal religion, then, focuses on the personal identity, an identity discovered through the story of the people of Israel but present in every Jewish life.

COVENANT AND THE PROPHETS

This idea of covenant as private obligations arising out of loyalty to the public good finds expression in the early sections of the prophets—in Joshua, Judges, Samuel, and Kings. It evolves from an emphasis on private duties, however, to an emphasis on the duties of leadership. Joshua 24, for example, stresses the primacy of religion as a force uniting a national community. Most scholars assume that the tradition revised in that story recalls the occasion on which Yahweh became the national deity for the Israelite people. While worship of a deity called Yahweh or Yahu may have preceded this event, that worship represented only local customs. In Joshua 24 the nation as a whole proclaims Yahweh as its exclusive God and thereby ratifies the laws of Yahweh as their "new constitution" in what the writer understood as a "covenant ceremony." Joshua 24 may be interpreted as "covenant ceremony" at which a "constitution" of Israel as a new nation was ratified. Although Joshua 24 in its present context appears to be a reaffirmation of the covenant made with Moses at Sinai, no reference to that covenant appears. Joshua notes that Israel's ancestors were idolaters. The Israelites must now, apparently for the first time, swear allegiance to Yahweh alone. Such an occasion could well have been the inauguration of independent Israelite nationhood. Scholars have long debated the exact meaning of the various covenant-making ceremonies found in the Book of Joshua. Commenting on them, Ernest Nicholson claims that "the idea of a cultic vow is absurd." He suggests, instead, that the book emphasizes national loyalties, particularly in contrast to an alliance with the Assyrian kingdom.[12] Covenant, understood in this context, represents the ideals of the community, a nation's self-understanding. Such a covenant reflects a society's cultural and spiritual identity.

This view of covenant as the basis for a society, as an expression of a nation's political vision, characterizes the entire second section of the Hebrew Bible, the Prophets. Covenant in this sense supplied a blueprint for social institutions, for national leaders, and for international decision-making. One of the earliest examples of such a use of covenant comes in 2 Samuel 7:8–16. God declares a covenant with the dynasty of King David. God promises to support that dynasty so each king may pursue a just social program. Covenant thus entails a unilateral commitment by the divine to a human king. The idea recurs often (see 2 Samuel 23:1–7 and Psalms 2:7–12, 72:1–17, 110, and 132). Thus Psalm 132:11–12 declares:

> The Lord swore to David an oath that he will not
>   break:
> A prince of your own line will I set upon your
>   throne.
> If your sons keep my covenant and heed my
>   covenant and heed the teaching that I give them
> Their sons in turn for all time shall sit upon your
>   throne.

Here covenant refers to the guidelines that Israel's leaders must follow. Rulers may expect national success and continued power only so long as they follow the social and political obligations set for them. Covenant, in this case, represents a check upon political power, on arbitrary government. This view of covenant, however, was honored more in the breach than in the practice. When that occurred, disaster often followed. In the wake of this pattern, individuals arose announcing a causal relationship between abandoning Torah teachings and the coming of disaster – the prophets. The prophet Amos declares (Amos 3:6–7) that evil does not befall a city unless the Lord has done it. Covenant forms the basis upon which Amos makes his statement. If the community organizes itself on the basis of divine commandments, it will succeed. If it follows an ungodly paradigm of political life, it will fail.

Not only Amos but other prophets as well utilize a peculiar form of address that scholars call the "covenant lawsuit." The covenant lawsuit form reproduces the covenant formulae and treaty language associated with the law codes in the Pentateuch. This legalistic view of Israel's obligations and responsibilities supports a particular form of prophetic address. They begin by calling the nation, or certain groups within the nation, to a judgment. They continue by describing the historical relationship between Israel and its God, emphasizing the obligations of that relationship. The lawsuit then notes how the defendant has not lived up to contractual duties and calls for a judgment. The judgment given usually points to a particular historical catastrophe that the prophet has predicted for the nation as a whole. While no evidence shows any other nation in the ancient Near East using this prophetic form, the lawsuit or treaty structure does follow a traditional structure, in this case one adapted from secular life by biblical prophets. Hosea uses this style against the kingdom of Israel (Hosea 4:1–3). He suggests that because "there is no faithfulness or kindness and no knowledge of God," natural and social disasters follow. God's actions, or better, the divine reactions to infractions of covenant obligations, affect the entire world order. Working backward, a prophet may deduce from the national, social and environmental situation whether the nation has fulfilled its covenantal duties.

The theme of that destruction raises ethical problems – note that the innocent animals suffer no less than the people. These problems became essential subject matter for the evolving religion of ancient Israel since history itself was thought to represent God's will and presence. Civil religion evokes the divine within history, as manifest in the fortunes of a particular nation. By observing the civil life of the community, then, theologians seek to deduce the nature of divinity. Covenant, from the perspective of its civil uses, suggests divine involvement in human politics.

COVENANT IN THE HEBREW WRITINGS

The third section of the Hebrew Bible often reiterates the ideas found in the previous sections. The royal covenant found in Psalm 132, for example, has already been noted. The national covenant, the civil religion of the Israelites, occurs as an explicit motif in various recitations of ancient history (see Nehemiah 9 and Psalms 47, 78, 105, and 147) and implicitly in a number of "cultic confessions" listing the covenant requirements for belonging to the Israelite community (see Psalms 15 and 24). A new note, however, emphasizes covenant as a means by which the Jewish community interacts with non-Jews. The most obvious example of this approach occurs in the covenantal ceremony attributed to Ezra at the time of the Jewish return to their land. This covenant emphasizes Jewish customs and endogamy, separatism and cultural distinctiveness (Ezra 9; Nehemiah 9–12). The same themes recur in books of the Writings such as Esther and Daniel. Other works, however, seem more general and universal in their teaching. Many of the psalms, most of the contents of Proverbs and Ecclesiastes, and the intention behind Job focus on general wisdom, on human truth applicable without distinction between cultures. Combining this universal theme with the parochial interests in other parts of the Writings suggests that when people use general wisdom to help structure their private (family) lives they will strengthen the community and will have exercised their civic duty. In such a case, civil law and personal living have become identified — an identification found in the last portions of this section of the Bible (Ezra 9; Nehemiah 10–13).

This new synthesis of personal and civil concerns creates a distinctive covenantal perspective. Whether Jews act according to general wisdom or to assert their national independence, they inevitably encounter non-Jews. Covenantal obligation, understood either as loyalty to national identity or the application of general wisdom, takes on meaning as a touchstone for relationships with the non-Jew. Works such as the First Book of Maccabees stress the differences between non-Jew and Jew; other writings such as the Fourth Book of Maccabees interpret Jewish life and belief in general philosophical (Greek) terms. Jacob Agus suggests the dynamic transformation of the idea of covenant reflected in this literature. He describes in detail the changes that occurred in Jewish life when Ezra, "with the express authorization of the Persian government," brought a new "sure covenant." Attention became focused on detail rather than on general theory.

Agus explains how the leaders of Jewry, the sages, sought to facilitate interaction between Jew and non-Jew, often through philosophical interpretations of Jewish teaching. Thus, a scholarly class developed that could explain the meaning of Judaism not only to a newly sophisticated Jewish elite but to non-Jews as well. The final result of such interpretation and study was, not unexpectedly, more universalist than the tradition had been until then. The Torah, that is, the essential obligations and expectations of covenantal religion, was claimed to entail "a set of universal principles applicable to all mankind," and Jewish teachers sought to bring all humanity "under the wings of the divine presence."[13] This emphasis changes covenant into a model for intergroup communication.

CIRCUMCISION AND TYPES OF COVENANTAL RELIGION

This interpretation of the biblical data according to the stipulative definition of covenant reveals three types of covenantal religion. In the first the obligations involved focus on a recitation of history, an acceptance of a self-image based upon an inherited tradition. The expectations flowing from these duties focus on a personal sense of worth, a reconciliation of one's individuality with the realities and facts of existence in a communal setting, and the promise that facing such reality results in a more productive life. Personal covenant, in this case, emphasizes each individual's search for identification. The second type of covenant emphasizes communal duties and the obligations of communal leaders. The expectations engendered center on community life — its success and prosperity, its responsiveness to challenges, its sensitivity to the needs of its members. Such a religion may be called "civil"; it understands covenant as the basis for civil organization. The third covenantal type establishes the framework for both individuals and groups who reach beyond their own communities. This type of universalistic covenant views obligation in terms of universal ideals and envisions in its expectations a transformation in the world as a whole. This universalistic covenant builds upon personal and civil distinctiveness to embrace all humanity.

This very general typology of covenant, as defined here, remains rather theoretical. Applying the formal definitions of this typology to a particular case demonstrates its characteristics more graphically. Rabbi Donin's interpretation of Jewish covenant seems to collapse when he turns his attention away from theology and toward specific Jewish practice. One such practice, that of *Brit Mila* or initiating a Jew into Jewish religion, illustrates his approach. The traditional ritual of infant circumcision represents an important part of Jewish life and an essential aspect of covenantal living. Not only is the ritual itself called "covenantal circumcision," but it acts as an initiation procedure by which infant males become part of the Jewish people. Lifsa Schachter, for example, analyzes the variety of biblical associations of the ritual and its manifestations in Jewish practice. Schachter contends that the ritual expresses basic Jewish ideals and proclaims "the goals of the covenant are the high social goals towards which Judaism was directed from its earliest days."[14] The variety of meanings given to that ritual exemplify the variety of covenantal forms.

One aspect of the ritual clearly emphasizes the individual and personal obligations. Jewish men undergo circumcision as the mark of their entry into covenantal life. In this way the ritual symbolizes obligations performed by individuals as they affirm their personal identity. By obeying precepts directed to them individually, each Jew discovers individual significance. In current practice, the ritual bears the name of the patriarch Abraham. Genesis 17 explains that God commanded Abraham to "walk before me and become whole," instituting the practice of circumcision as a means to that end. Despite other indications in the Hebrew Bible (Exodus 4, for example), the association of circumcision with the commandment to Abraham remains central in Jewish thinking. Even the great covenant at Sinai, Exodus 19–20, may be interpreted with reference to circumcision. Nicholson contends that the covenant of circumcision remains a constant presence even when not mentioned in that later narrative. Thus he suggests that the "blood consecration" does not make the nation a kinfolk, but rather, as in the case of the priesthood, blood purifies and makes those who share in it holy. Understood in this way, circumcision provides a type of sanctification by which each individual attains holiness.[15]

Circumcision, however, also serves a communal purpose. When the Israelite slaves prepare for liberation from Egyptian bondage, they are told the laws of communal life, including the laws of circumcision. These laws establish the boundaries of the community and determine who will be considered an Israelite and who will share in the success of the community. On the basis of this text, it might be assumed that the Passover ritual that preceded redemption from Egypt required all male participants to be circumcised. The Hebrew Bible, in contrast to the Septuagint translation, takes this Passover and circumcision ritual as a fact of history. When Joshua circumcises the

Israelites in Joshua 5, then, the Hebrew Bible must make this a "second circumcision" (thus in modern Jewish practice there are two stages to ritual circumcision). The duplication of rituals, however, probably arose in the editing of the Hebrew Bible, during which time the event took on a covenantal meaning. One modern scholar notes that the passage makes no mention of covenant, but the idea is clearly "at the very heart of the subject."[16]

This allusion to covenant may result from an editor's feeling that one type of circumcision — that of the individual as expressed in Genesis 17 — did not exhaust the meaning of the concept; as a covenant symbol circumcision needed to include a communal reference. As the concept of covenant agreement evolves to greater and wider significance, so too the interpretation of circumcision as its symbol develops its broader implications.

The references to Abraham and Joshua refer to the Israelites themselves. Very often, however, circumcision appears to be a means of distinguishing the Israelites from others. The author of 1 Maccabees indicates the assimilation of the Judean priests by remarking that "they removed their mark of circumcision and repudiated the holy covenant" (1 Maccabees 1:15). From this perspective circumcision acts as a barrier to separate Jew from non-Jew, as a distinctive mark of Judaic identity that prevents assimilation with the general culture.

This association of circumcision, covenant, and identity had already been recognized by Spinoza, who attributed Jewish survival to this practice. While Spinoza insisted that the Bible provides civil and ceremonial law (and not theological truth), nevertheless he considered that civil law peculiarly effective. Were Jews to regain their nation, he predicted, they could, through the ritual of circumcision, restore their entire social order. As a mark of cultural distinctiveness, circumcision allows Jews to interact with others without losing their identity.[17]

Covenant, understood this way, entails those actions by which Jews maintain their own particular identity in the face of temptations to assimilate with others. Such distinctiveness, however, need not lead to chauvinism. While 1 Maccabees emphasizes this point, other traditions do not. The author of Daniel, for example, may be understood as a pacifist who opposes Maccabean militancy. Thus Daniel 11:32–34 may respond to the Maccabean policy of forced circumcision. While Jews who abandon the covenant are disloyal, those who impose it on others are "overzealous."[18] Circumcision may be a means by which Jews maintain their loyalty to tradition without at the same time being alienated from other nations. Philo understands this point and explains circumcision in general philosophical terms. He claims that circumcision merely symbolizes the conquering of passion—a universal human virtue that takes on a peculiar symbolism in Judaism but should not separate Jews from non-Jews.[19] Such a theory means that while circumcision might serve a useful social function among Jews, it should not interfere with relationships among Jews and non-Jews. Hellenistic views of Jewish proselytism took this view seriously. Potential converts were urged to accept Jewish ethical teachings without fulfilling the requirement for circumcision. The unusual cases in which that ritual took place were considered extraordinary and, from a faith perspective, unessential.[20] Circumcision, in this understanding, merely symbolizes Jewish ideas—ideas on the basis of which Jews and non-Jews can meet in a single covenant community. The ritual of circumcision, then, may be understood as a tool to allow Jewish interaction with non-Jews while preventing complete assimilation to non-Jewish ways.

The differences between covenantal religion in Deuteronomy 26, Joshua 5, and 1 Maccabees 1 reinforces the typology already suggested. In the first type covenantal obligations fall upon the individual, and covenantal promises are directed to the individual. Covenant entails a philosophy of individualism, of personal difference, of private identities, promising rewards for fidelity to individual talents. It also establishes certain deeds that distinguish those who follow them from others and provides specific rewards for such actions. The common ground between the divine and the human lies in the sphere of personal action and private commitment.

The second type of covenantal religion, however, focuses on beliefs about the community, a philosophy of social rather than personal identity, suggesting the value of a particular social organization. This second type includes a set of behavioral injunctions that falls upon the collectivity as a whole, a code of civil regulations, obedience to which brings benefits to the society as a whole. The common ground of human and divine activity, in this case, becomes political. God demands a certain type of social order and protects that social order.

The final type of covenantal religion evinces a more global awareness. This religion establishes beliefs about one collectivity in its relations with others; its philosophy is international rather than merely national. The precepts inculcated concern the interaction of nations, the dialogue between communities, the respective independence of divergent groups. God meets humanity, in this case, when human communities interact. God's concern extends beyond a single society to embrace all societies.

COVENANTAL RELIGION AND MODERN JEWS

Jews have traditionally embraced all three types of covenantal religion, although sometimes focusing exclusively on one or another of them. Modern Jews, however, have found each of the three types problematic in the modern world. David Hartman correctly recognizes the crisis of modern Judaism as "the loss of a shared value framework for translating our historical consciousness into present experiences," and, again I think correctly, suggests that "covenant" offers a useful theological solution to that crisis.[21] He notes that modern Jews find themselves caught between equally unacceptable alternatives of submission to authority or personal self-assertion, of social concern or inner-directed faith, of messianic nationalism or messianic internationalism. Covenant, however, emphasizes both human potential as partners with God and the need for human self-restraint — God's plan, not human desires, sets the agenda for human action. Hartman demonstrates that a number of contemporary Jewish dilemmas — religion in the state of Israel, the meaning of Jewish prayer, the flexibility of Jewish law — may be resolved when the implications of covenant have been made clear.

Hartman's approach, while always provocative and suggestive, often falls short of revitalizing the theological terminology and traditional texts utilized. Hartman draws eclectically from the entire Jewish tradition, investigates medieval and modern Jewish thought, and offers the reflections of a traditional Jew encountering the challenge of modernity. He does not, however, at least in the book quoted here, suggest the principles of obligation and expectation, sketch the "common ground" with the deity, or categorize types of covenantal existence needed to refashion this concept as a theoretical category. This study takes up just that challenge.

NOTES

1.   See the discussion by Jon D. Levenson, "Covenant and Commandment," *Tradition* 21 (1983), pp. 42–51. Levenson notes the strangeness of the concept in Judaism and its rooting in modern Christian theology. He also shows the variety of covenantal models found in the Hebrew Bible. Compare Dennis J. McCarthy, *Old Testament Covenant: A Survey of Current Opinions*, Growing Points in Theology Series (Richmond: John Knox, 1972); Ernest W. Nicholson, *God and His People: Covenant and Theology in the Old Testament* (Oxford: Clarendon Press, 1986); David Novak, "The Logic of the Covenant: An Essay in Systematic Jewish Theology," in *Halakhah in a Theological Dimension* (Chico, California: Scholars Press, 1985), pp. 116–31; David Sperling, "Israel's Religion in the Ancient Near East," in *Jewish Spirituality: From the Bible Through the Middle Ages*, ed. Arthur Green (New York: Crossroad, 1986), pp. 5–31.

2.   David Hartman's sustained analysis *A Living Covenant: The Innovative Spirit in Traditional Judaism* (New York: The Free Press, 1985) offers a useful alternative to models such as legalism, traditionalism, or

submission as a means of understanding Judaism. He may well have discovered a useful metaphor for combining human dignity with recognition of divine power. Whether that paradigm in fact represents the models utilized in the biblical tradition, however, may be argued, as he himself understands.

3.   Hayim Halevy Donin, *To Be a Jew: A Guide to Jewish Observance in Contemporary Life* (New York: Basic Books, 1972), pp. 19, 22, 273–76.

4.   Richard Robinson, *Definition* (Oxford: Clarendon Press, 1950), pp. 29, 66; see the useful argument throughout the book.

5.   Ibid., pp. 149–92. I am indebted to my colleague Robert N. Minor for drawing my attention to this valuable study.

6.   McCarthy, *Old Testament Covenant*, p. 85.

7.   Steven T. Katz, *Jewish Ideas and Concepts* (New York: Schocken, 1977), p. 161; see his entire discussion on pp. 156–62.

8.   Jacob Bernard Agus, *The Evolution of Jewish Thought* (New York: Abelard-Schuman, 1959), p. 416.

9.   Gerhard von Rad, *Studies in Deuteronomy*, Studies in Biblical Theology no. 9 (London: SCM Press, 1953), p. 23; von Rad, *Deuteronomy: A Commentary* (Philadelphia: Westminster, 1966), pp. 157–62.

10.   Novak, "The Logic of the Covenant."

11.   Will Herberg, *Judaism and Modern Man: An Interpretation of Jewish Religion* (New York: Harper and Row, 1951), p. 271.

12.   Nicholson, *God and His People*, pp. 154–55.

13.   Agus, *Evolution*, pp. 47–67.

14.   Lifsa Schachter, "Reflections on the Brit Mila Ceremony," *Conservative Judaism* 38:4 (1986), pp. 38–41.

15.   Nicholson, *God and His People*, pp. 171–72.

16.   J. Alberto Scoggin, *Joshua: A Commentary*, trans. by R. A. Wilson (Philadelphia: Westminster, 1972), p. 70.

17.   Benedict de Spinoza, *Theologico-Political Treatise*, trans. R. H. M. Elwes (New York: Dover, 1951), pp. 54–56.

18.   See *I Maccabees: A New Translation With Introduction and Commentary by Jonathan A. Goldstein*, Anchor Series (Garden City, New York: Doubleday, 1976), pp. 200–201; see also *The Book of Daniel: A New Translation With Introduction and Commentary by Louis F. Hartman and Alexander A. Di Lella*, Anchor Series (Garden City, New York: Doubleday, 1978), pp. 299–301.

19.   See the discussion in Samuel Sandmel, *Philo's Place in Judaism: A Study of Conceptions of Abraham in Jewish Literature* (New York: Ktav, 1971), pp. 147, 160.

20.   See the analysis of Josephus' view on the relationship of circumcision and conversion in Lawrence H. Schiffman, "The Conversion of the

Royal House of Abiabene in Josephus and Rabbinic Sources," in *Josephus, Judaism, and Christianity*, ed. Louis H. Feldman and Gohei Hata (Detroit: Wayne State University Press, 1987), pp. 302–8.

21.   Hartman, *Living Covenant*, p. 17.

2

The Crisis of Covenant

EXPECTATIONS, OBLIGATIONS, AND MODERN COVENANTAL RELIGION

Modern Jews often reject the obligations inherited from traditional religion, contend that the expectations promised by that religion are unpersuasive, and refuse to identify traditional Jewish activities as those in which the divine and human share. While people in pre-modern times presumed the primacy of the group and its culture, modernity — since at least the eighteenth century — has presumed the centrality of the individual. How can a contemporary person affirm the value and authority of an inherited religious tradition while still maintaining the personal authenticity and independence that is the hallmark of modernity? That question shapes the way modern religious leaders have thought about religion and theology. An early Jewish leader of the nineteenth century, Rabbi Yosef (Yossel) Horwitz, became an exponent of the Musar Movement, a movement attempting to revitalize the meaning of Judaism by focusing on the life of the individual. The term "rabbi" implies that Yossel served the community not by performing rituals but by teaching. Such teaching often entailed making legal decisions, but more often included instructing students in the process of Jewish law. As a leading rabbi, Yossel had the responsibility of teaching young Jews the entire Jewish legal tradition — its classical sources, its codified volumes, its collected case material. As a religious figure he sought to instill in them a passion for the meaning and purpose of this tradition. He combined teaching a subject matter — Jewish law — with conveying an attitude — obedience to this law provides an answer to the question of life's meaning.

One story shows that he was attuned to the particular problems of the modern world. According to this story, Rabbi Yossel had a prize pupil. This pupil had come to study with him from a distant village, consumed by a passion for knowledge. Day and night the student devoted his efforts to mastering the texts of traditional Judaism. The student appeared driven by questions that needed answers, and Rabbi Yossel assured him that the Jewish tradition would supply those answers. Three times a year the pupil would interrupt his study, leave the confines of Rabbi Yossel's school, and return home. On one such trip he began a discussion with his friends. At first he tried to interest them in the text he had mastered. Slowly they convinced him that truth lay not in traditional answers but in the secular process of raising questions. The student turned aside from tradition when he found the questions of modernity more intriguing than the answers of received texts.

Rabbi Yossel took this lesson to heart and changed his way of teaching and even his curriculum.[1] The importance of his example lies less in the corrective measures he took than in his recognition of the problem. The difficulties confronting modern Jews examining covenantal religion exceed those of previous generations and pervade each of the three types of covenantal obligations and expectations noted in the first chapter. Rabbi Yossel's student rejected traditional views of his duties and obligations because they no longer compelled his assent. They failed to provide him with a consistent sense of identity, with a secure communal environment, or with an adequate means of reaching out to non-Jews in his society. The modern crisis for contemporary Jewry resembles that of Rabbi Yossel's disciple: covenantal religion no longer seems able to supply the personal, social, or generally human needs of their lives.

PROBLEMS IN COVENANT AS PERSONAL IDENTITY

Many Jews conclude that traditional Judaism cannot provide a compelling and persuasive world view for modern women and men. Will Herberg describes the plight of humanity today as "at the brink of the abyss with all our supports swept away," and he includes "conventional ethics and religion" among those foundations no longer standing.[2] Modern Jews look to covenantal religion as a solution to their crisis of identity, but often find it an unsatisfactory answer. Modern Jews seek to find in their past a clue to their meaning in the present. To solve that problem, however, they need a stronger sense of the present than that provided by contemporary Jewish life.

A story told of one of the early masters, Rabbi Bunam, suggests that this new concern confronted Jews at the very beginning of the modern period. According to the tale, a student approached the rabbi, wishing to study with him. The rabbi demanded to know what he had come to achieve. The student answered that he wished to search for God. "God," the rabbi replied, "can be found anywhere. You do not need to come to me to learn how to seek for God. Come to me only if you wish to search for yourself. When you have learned to know yourself, then you can find the divine, as Job 17:15 intimates — from myself I shall see God."[3] The quest for God, this text suggests, must begin as a search for the self.

While the basic task requires introspection, such inwardness need not be a passive self-indulgence. The creation of a modern Jewish self-consciousness requires effort and activism. This call for activism echoes the traditional song attributed to Moses and the Israelites when crossing the Sea of Reeds (Exodus 15:2). The Hebrews, rejoicing at their newly won freedom, declare, "This is my God whom I will beautify, my ancestral God whom I will praise." Only an activist orientation that takes responsibility for discovering God personally can lay the foundation for an affirmation of traditional religion.

A Hasidic rabbi interprets this biblical verse so that its

activist position becomes even more explicit.[4] The rabbi derives the verb in the first phrase from a Hebrew word meaning "place." On this understanding the verse can read: "This is my God for whom I shall make a place." This means that before Jews can appropriate their ancestral tradition they must first prepare a place within themselves for that God. Certainly some Jews begin with their inherited tradition. Others, however, need to look first within themselves, must discover ways in which they can internalize their Jewishness. Making this personal question central, however, represents a departure from the tradition.

As modern Jews pursue this active search for personal meaning, they find that Jewish tradition offers very little help. Jewish philosophy represents the views of different Jews in different cultural and intellectual environments. The definition of Jewish identity supplied by Judah Halevi conflicts with that generated by Moses Maimonides. Among modern Jewish thinkers the divergence is, if anything, even greater than that among earlier Jewish philosophers. Many important modern thinkers have been Jews. Does that accident of birth stamp their thinking as "Jewish"? Formalists declare that any statement by any Jew is thereby Jewish. Essentialists declare that only those statements that reflect "true" Judaism are Jewish, without regard to the identity of the author. Raphael Jospe summarizes these debates on whether Jewish philosophy may be distinguished by its content or by its authors. Is a way of thinking Jewish because of what it says or because of who does the thinking? He argues cogently that "when it comes to determining Jewishness, we must consider the speaker and not what is said."[5] Covenant obligations are those that determine "Jewishness" and as such belong to the "formal" rather than the "essentialist" category. The first challenge to modern Jewish thinking, then, must be how to enable individual Jews to discover their Jewishness, that is, the nature of the inherent and inherited aspects of themselves that lead them and others to identify them as Jews. Since this Jewishness is a given (a "supernatural fact," in the words of Will Herberg), it can be discovered only by examining the facticity – the concrete existential situation of modern Jews. Modern Jews confront the dilemma of Rabbi Yossel's pupil when they examine their own sense of reality and of Judaism.

THE SOCIAL ASPECT OF COVENANT AND MODERNITY

The second type of covenantal religion fails no less than the first. Modern Jews find an affirmation of covenant as civil religion equally problematic as that of covenant as personal identity. Traditionally, covenantal obligations have been understood as communal ones: creating societal mechanisms that preserve space for Jewish living. The spheres of private and public life interact with each other. Traditional Judaism consists of a series of "concentric levels" of public and private, communal and individual, and ethnic and universal concerns, all interconnecting.[6]

Modernity separates these concentric spheres and partitions lives so that obligations to family, nation, and ethnic group often conflict with one another. The experience of the modern Jew has usually been one of "marginality." This social situation leaves individuals and groups on the fringes of the major institutions and civil organizations of society. Jews as individuals and as a group face alienation and exclusion from the social structures of the majority culture. Through adaptation and assimilation both can become more acceptable to that culture. Nevertheless, such self-transformation leaves Jews impoverished culturally. Attempted remedies, however, "do not appear to have been either substantial or particularly effective."[7] Jews find civil covenant as difficult to affirm as Jewish identity.

Creating a place for the institutions of Judaism, especially in a time that has experienced Auschwitz and the reborn Jewish state, entails renewing the social institutions of Jewry. Modern

Jews have not abandoned the public sphere, but they have transformed it. Modern Jewish communal life exhibits its own form of rituals, its own set of social obligations, its own cultural expressions. Traditional Jews often disparage the novel creations of such modern responses. Other students of modern Jewry, however, acknowledge that these responses have often been highly successful. Jacob Neusner notes the enduring pattern of Jewish living that American Jews have invented. He recognizes their value as "ways of being Jewish" that persist "for five or six or more" generations.[8] Finding a place for Judaism includes legitimating the new approaches Jews have constructed to their social and communal life. While the Jewish tradition offers guidelines for Jewish behavior and social action, the modern Jew finds it difficult to passively accept traditional directives. The older models of rabbi, messiah, or autonomous ethnic community no longer compel Jewish belief; newer models of pure nationalism or religious belief tend to lack traditional approbation.

Some Jews affirm nationalism, or better, the creation of a national consciousness, as their primary goal. They see this consciousness as a way to cope with this problem of social experimentation without relinquishing traditional symbolism. The recent history of the Jewish people makes such a recognition problematic. During World War II the Nazis slaughtered six million Jews. After the war, the rise of the State of Israel convinced some Jews that only military force and secularism could protect Jewry. The tragic lessons of Israel's modern history, which include the dangers of being either victims or victimizers, suggest to some Jewish thinkers that there may be no place for Judaism in modern history at all. Others insist that Judaism must make itself a place in the modern world as a heroic response to that history. The answer has not been decided, but Eliezer Berkovits correctly notes the dual heritage of modern Jews. On the one hand, they inherit the rebellion of those who refuse to grant Judaism a place in modern history. On the other hand, they confront the witness of those testifying to the enduring power of Jewish commitment.[9]

Jewish communal identity becomes problematic not only because the holocaust suggests that diaspora models of Judaism are inadequate. Zionism, a new model of political life, proves just as difficult to affirm. It often restricts rather than broadens the range of human interaction. One Jewish theologian voiced concern over just this problem — Martin Buber. Some of Buber's most profoundly moving writings focus on what has been considered the tragedy of the Middle East: the relationship between the Jews and the non-Jewish Arab population.[10] Buber spoke to a community emerging from the return itself. The agony of the dilemma springs from a conflict of rights. Just as Jews needed (and still need) a home of their own, a land on which to carry forward the divine experiment mandated by their religion, so too do those who are already on the land. During the pre-State period Buber was among those who argued against a national Jewish state and in favor of a binational state, claiming that while the upbuilding of Zion required an immigration of Jews, a political Jewish majority was neither essential nor desirable. Many modern Jews agree with Buber, but rather than evolve an alternative to David Ben Gurion's Zionism, they reject covenantal religion, understood as a set of political obligations and expectations creating a society in which the divine and the human share, as a racist paradigm abrogating the rights of minorities.

JUDAISM AND A PLURALISTIC WORLD

The covenantal model of Jewish relationships with non-Jews also presents problems for contemporary Jews. They confront a universe in which they coexist with non-Jews, in which parochial religion cannot survive. Modern religion depends upon an open attitude towards others, a willingness to discover faith through interaction with those who do not share our own commitments. As Jacob Agus notes, the "double orientation" of modern faith emphasizes the reality of "outer facts" dependent upon listening to others, and "inner truth" emerging from within the soul.[11] The new Jewish identity that Jews discover, the new communities they form, the new responsibilities they accept, must encourage a reaching out to others rather than an isolationist attitude.

Many Jews envision their covenantal task in universal terms. The general malaise of modern society challenges them to correct its flaws and reform its errors. Understood this way covenant obligates every Jew to participate in the wider society. Covenantal expectations and obligations direct Jewish personal and social living. The divine and the human participate in a cosmic endeavor of *tikkun olam*, the improvement of the world. Rabbi Hayim Halevy Donin, for example, argues persuasively that in a time when Jews face "competing ideologies and movement" they must demonstrate Torah as "a relevant philosophy and way of life capable of challenging the various 'isms' and spiritual fads that from time to time sweep across our society."[12] He offers Jewish religion as a hopeful harbinger of peace to all humanity.

Despite his advocacy of Jewish teachings as a solution to modern social dilemmas, Rabbi Donin must admit that the various laws of the Torah do indeed separate Jews from other people. The covenantal obligations and expectations that identify Jews as members of a particular community also isolate them from others. The combination of a universal intent with a particularistic reality leaves Judaism as exclusivist, dogmatic, and alienating.

Modern Jews find it hard to accept such an exclusivist and particularistic tradition. While the Torah insists that Jews are to be a priestly people who model ideal behavior for others, most modern Jews see their distinctiveness as an obstacle, not a stepping stone to intercommunal dialogue. Jacob Agus notes that within any single tradition, some adherents look beyond its past to the future while others submit to the past as a fixed standard. He distinguishes between those members who "sense its living tensions and those for whom the sanctified solutions of the past are sufficient."[13] Some Jews urge that the tradition remain within its self-enclosed isolation. Other Jews call for a complete integration with the general culture. Neither offers a sufficient nor realistic answer to the challenge of modernity. Unless the third type of covenantal religion can extend beyond a mere acceptance, even celebration, of human differences and point to a transcending of them, many Jews will reject its appeal. Modernity challenges every aspect of covenantal religion, whether understood as creating a personal world view, a civil religion, or a framework for international human relationships.

JEWISH RELIGION TODAY: THE CRITIQUE OF RICHARD RUBENSTEIN

The three challenges before contemporary Jewish religion have been sketched in rather general terms. A more intense and developed critique comes from Richard L. Rubenstein, whose evolving interpretation of modernity and religion reveals the basic problems within covenantal thought. He has carried his critique to its logical extreme: modernity requires Jews to abandon their traditional views of God and the Jewish people. They may be able to reconstruct a new religiosity, but it will take a very different shape from that suggested either by covenantal models or traditional paradigms.

Rubenstein suggests that the experience Jews have had in the modern world leads to an inevitable rejection of the covenantal world view, its communal paradigms, and its monotheistic model. Three aspects of contemporary Jewish experience have made traditional Jewish covenantal religion indefensible: the facticity of the Jewish people, the untenability of Jewish institutional models, and the parochial nature of the covenantal model. The mythic stories Jews affirm cannot match the realities of Jewish national existence in a world that has slaughtered six million Jews and in which a Jewish national home must fight to preserve its very existence. The twin

paradigms of covenantal institutions of law and royal preroga-
tives of power cannot answer the problems of a modern nation
state. The covenantal model tends to isolate and segregate Jews
from non-Jews and thus cannot address the world community
in which all human beings today must learn to live.

THE HOLOCAUST, ISRAEL, AND THE FACTICITY
OF JEWISH LIFE

Rubenstein contends that modern life has made the facticity
of Jewish life an unalterable basis for any theologizing. Not
only the tragic facticity of Nazi persecution but also the glorious
facticity of a new Jewish state represents a new Jewish sensibility. Rubenstein celebrates the "new paganism" he finds in
contemporary Jewish life.[14] He applauds this new religion "in
which the aspirations, the hopes, the tragedies, and the guilts
of the human condition can be continuously and meaningfully
shared" and castigates theologians who insist on retelling the
Jewish story in old ways.[15]

Rubenstein suggests that Arthur A. Cohen, a contemporary
Jewish thinker, misunderstands the true goal of Jewish
theologizing and forgets that theology must tell a story that
corresponds to the social and communal reality of a living
people. The true agenda must be to "help create a true community of persons rooted in human solidarity and helpful-
ness."[16] A less realistic approach will lead inevitably to disaster.
Those who reiterate the older myths run the risks of repeating
the history of the holocaust because they ignore the lessons
taught by modern history. Jews who rely on older models of
identity may expect history to follow those paradigms, leading
to disaster for Jewish survival. Rubenstein admits that individuals need to have myths as a means of understanding and
conceptualizing reality. He merely suggests that the traditional
Jewish myths fail to offer a helpful vision of the world in a
post-holocaust time. The expectations and obligations that
define Jewish identity must meet a modern criterion of realism.

The realism that focused Rubenstein's attention on "neo-paganism" and on Jewish parochialism led him to a new insight. The facticity of human life today cannot be restricted to a narrow nationalism. Not only are the myths of Judaism unhistorical and unfactual, they also prevent the development of an extended community of human interaction that should be the aim of responsible theologians. Such a community must express a wider religious viewpoint than that provided by a parochial national mythology. The story of Israel's covenant beginnings by traditional Judaism, a story that emphasizes exclusiveness rather than inclusiveness, precludes creating a universal religious community. God appears to glory in favoritism, to choose one nation and reject others, to protect the chosen ones from harm and disaster, a view of deity clearly inappropriate for a community that has suffered the horrors of the holocaust.

Rubenstein himself suggests a different model of divinity arising from contemporary Jewish experience. Divinity may be destructive as well as creative; God may be the "Holy Nothing" from which all things come and to which all must return. Only a self-understanding that grows out of this new universalism, out of the experience of the identity of all victims, can hope to be adequate to modern life. The advantage of such a view of God, rooted in the facticity of contemporary experience, transcends its application to Jews. God as "Holy Nothingness" has been "known to mystics of all ages." The religious view of such a theology has much in common with "atheistic existentialists such as Sartre and Camus" and reflects the common human experience, not merely Jewish experience. Rubenstein claims that because it mirrors the universal human predicament, the vulnerable human condition, the religious community offers "the institution in which that condition can be shared in depth." Such a sharing represents an extension of Jewish identity to include all victims of modernity.[17] A new Judaism must evolve more realistic obligations and expectations of personal covenant and must universalize the notion of how those obligations and expectations interact with divinity.

A CRITIQUE OF JEWISH INSTITUTIONAL MODELS

Rubenstein's thinking moves beyond the rejection of theological myth to reject the various institutional forms of Jewish life suggested in traditional sources. He recognizes the diversity of Jewish options but claims that none are satisfying. The Bible, for example, seems to emphasize two institutional paradigms, each disguised as an absolute ideal.[18] One model, the covenantal model associated with the revelation at Mount Sinai, inculcates institutional humility. Only God controls human life, destiny, and behavior. The institutions of society act as instruments of divine control over the world and as such must subordinate their particular needs to God's overall plan. No human power holds the final authority; all institutions merely serve a temporary tenancy under the grace of the divine. This model suggests an institutional democracy — leaders serve a certain constituency, they function less as independent political figures than as servants of the community, even the most despotic of institutions actually follow a preordained rather than self-propelled course. Jewish institutions, priestly, prophetic, or pedagogical, need not be autonomous, independent forces. They can compromise with foreign powers and governments because temporal authority merely masks divine activity. Such an approach allows Jewish institutions to cooperate with non-Jewish forces by suggesting the divine authority sanctions these powers, thus rationalizing both Jewish powerlessness as equal to (although more apparent than) that of the great global leaders.

Rubenstein claims that this Sinaitic model would be "most likely to arise in the aftermath of a natural or social catastrophe." Rubenstein credits this theory with enabling Judaism "to maintain its religious and communal integrity in the face of repeated military and political catastrophes."[19] This ideology and its institutions might help in coping with the crisis of the holocaust. One might argue, then, that the ideology of Sinai proves remarkably useful to the modern Jew seeking to cope with political helplessness. The Nazis, however, made good use of these types of institutions to help run their death camps; a strategy that once permitted Jews to survive became a means for helping their enemies slaughter them. The Judenrat, the internal Jewish communal leadership, collaborated with the Germans — not in bad faith but because of an ideological institutional commitment that failed to meet Jewish needs.[20]

Even in biblical times, Rubenstein contends, the limits of this model had been discovered since it contains within itself the seeds of its own destruction. By its very nature, the covenantal paradigm thrives on social instability, undermines authority, and becomes dysfunctional in times when secure and predictable policies are needed. An alternative ideology arises to meet the new needs of more certain times. Rubenstein suggests that the biblical contention of sacral kingship came to replace covenantal thinking. Sacral kingship interpreted the community in terms of the power of the state. Whereas the Exodus paradigm interpreted social obligations and expectations in terms of inner freedom and the rule of law, the royal paradigm interpreted them in authoritarian ways, emphasizing obedience to established power and the maintenance of civil stability.

Not insignificantly, civil order and the centrality of national existence play major roles in Rubenstein's view of Zionism in the modern age. The difference between the ancient paradigm and the modern one, however, should not be forgotten. Traditional Jewish institutions absolutized the paradigms they exemplified. The sacral kingship legitimated itself by an appeal to the deity. Rubenstein denies that such a mythic view of institutions can aid Jewish survival. Indeed this myth may be more pernicious than the Exodus myth since it elevates a parochial identity above humanitarian concerns. Rubenstein realizes that almost every communal myth must be a civil religion and suggests the potentials for abuse within much civil religiosity. The obligations and expectations of Jewish civil life, however, seem limiting and often self-defeating. Calling those limitations the "common ground" of the divine and human encourages the very destructiveness that Jews have experienced so often in their communal existence.

MYTH, PAROCHIALISM, AND THE NEED FOR A NEW ETHIC

The way in which Rubenstein analyzes Jewish ideas shows his distance from traditional Judaic thought. By putting both the paradigm of covenant and that of sacral kingship under the microscope of sociological investigation, he demonstrates that neither provides a compelling ideology for today. The light of objective study reveals that these patterns of self-presentation lack intrinsic merit and are valid only insofar as they serve a social use. Rubenstein cannot take comfort in a traditional language even if he recognizes its power. His rationalism unmasks its weaknesses. As one interpreter understands it, Rubenstein's work is marked by a distinctive alienation from traditional mythic language. His inability to utilize the inherited ideology sets him apart from other modern Jewish thinkers.[21]

This rejection of mythology accompanies a rejection of inherited Jewish ethics. Rubenstein claims that scholarly investigation proves the ideology reflects a political pragmatism, not an ontological reality. Naive belief, acceptable in the past, becomes criminal in the light of the lessons of the holocaust. Modern history illustrates the dominance of social, economic, and psychological causes of religious belief; thus, modern Jews have forfeited their critical skills. Rubenstein rejects belief in the supremacy of a transcendent God whose inscrutable ways cannot be questioned as a condemnation to repeat recent history. He claims that "the community of men is possible only through the encounter of persons rather than of myths or abstractions."[22] Modern Jews who fail to understand that lesson continue to delude themselves and others, with tragic results.

A mythic tradition, Rubenstein argues, undermines an ability to respond realistically to political threats. Humanity must demythologize its world view to avoid the hostility, primitive hatreds, and self-deception that will lead to future holocausts.

While Rubenstein's earliest writings on the holocaust focus on the unique theological challenge it poses, his later writings see the Nazi program of extermination of Jews as an example of the unique possibilities of modernity. The radical challenge of contemporary life means that old models of religion no longer serve a useful purpose. While elements of Judaism may be of value to humanity, the monotheistic premise that Judaism should provide a single religion for humanity can only isolate and segregate Jews in a time when unity must be created.

The holocaust represents a unique stage in the development of humanity, one necessary step in the demonic rationalization process leading to a demythologized world controlled by impersonal social forces. After centuries of progress in scientific and dispassionate social control, he contends, "something happened in the twentieth century that made it morally and psychologically possible to realize dreams of destructiveness that had previously been confined to fantasy."[23] Thus Rubenstein suggests that the holocaust represents a new historical reality, a reality that permits human beings to commit legal genocide without qualms of legality or conscience. He marshals the facts of the holocaust in connection with descriptions of other twentieth-century inhumanities to show how economic necessity, sociological imperatives, psychological pressures, and the process of rationality combine to undermine the restraining power of traditional values. In a world attuned to efficiency and expediency, human beings become expendable for the sake of social engineering.[24] The holocaust teaches that modernity makes any minority radically vulnerable to ideological attack. Only a new sense of community that extends beyond Jewish exclusivism can prevent a continuation of the social and political atrocities that have marked modernity.

Rubenstein's call for a new sense of community arises from his rejection of traditional values and ethics, the myth and ideology on which he places much of the blame for modern problems. He utilizes the Jewish mythic story as a prototype — here was a "people who shared neither common origin nor religious inheritance" who did indeed evolve a religious consensus.[25] The Jewish story, however, is not the only one to fit this pattern. Christianity and Confucian religion also provide examples of such religious consensus. Judaism taken alone appears too limited, too parochial, too insular. He calls instead for a "global civilization" that intertwines Moses, Mohammed, Christ, and Confucius.[26] Jewish mythology must be replaced by a universal ethical religion for humanity as a whole. Jews must learn to admit that they represent but one part of religious humanity or they bankrupt their covenantal paradigm. Exclusivism and self-differentiation exacerbate rather than heal modern problems and thereby delegitimate the religion associated with them.

TOWARDS A NEW VIEW OF JEWISH COVENANT

Rubenstein's three criticisms challenge the basis of Jewish covenantal thinking. The individual Jew must learn to refashion the expectations and obligations associated with Jewish identity in order to claim that personal selfhood develops in partnership with that God responsible for the facticity of modern experience. Jewish institutions need to reconstrue both their sense of task and their religious justification lest they become either irrelevant or dangerous to the survival of the Jewish people. Jewish theology, with its emphasis on Jewish exclusivism, even if couched in universalist language, must rethink its relationship to other cultures and enter into interhuman dialogue.

Judaism provides precedent for such a renewal. Jewish philosophers and theologians in the past have reconstructed Jewish ideas. In the eighteenth century one such leader, Rabbi Menaham Mendel of Kotzk, led his disciples to radically reevaluate Jewish ideas. Many modern Jewish thinkers have turned to the Kotzker as an example of radical religious life. Elie Wiesel finds his teachings useful in discovering the meaning of modern identity; Martin Buber discerns the shape of true community in his writings; Abraham Heschel compares him to Soren Kierkegaard as an exemplar of that type of "depth-theology" expressing the common human situation. In each case the Kotzker provides a key to reconstructing the covenant-models of Jewish life. While Wiesel, Buber, and Heschel each have particular theologies of their own, their use of the Kotzker offers a helpful image of how covenant has been reshaped by modern thinkers, just as the Kotzker's own philosophy shows a dynamic Jewish self-renewal in process.[27]

Rabbi Menahem Mendel Morgenstern, known more generally as the Rebbe of Kotzk, often called the Kotzker, was born in Poland in 1783. According to the stories, even when young he had an unsociable personality, which led to the nickname "Black Mendel." As a teenager he left the traditional legalism of his family and attached himself to a mystical master, the Hasidic rabbi known as the Seer of Lublin. Despite this choice, however, he remained restless and unsatisfied. His criticism of other leaders estranged him from them. His writings demonstrate a bitter rejection of all his colleagues and contemporaries, a rejection that finally alienated him from his own students. One Sabbath eve in 1840, according to several pupils explaining why they left him to establish their own community, Rabbi Menahem Mendel declared himself a heretic. Other disciples, however, remained loyal to the Kotzker and denied the accusation. Whatever may have happened, Menahem Mendel secluded himself from both his followers and opponents for the next nineteen years until his death in 1859.

The Kotzker's primary aim seems to have been that of building a world, establishing a cosmos. A well-known story associated with him illustrates this goal. Once the Kotzker was visited by a colleague who had been a fellow student of the Holy Yehudi of Pshyskhe. The Kotzker demanded, "Yankl, why was man created on this earth?" "He was created in order to restore the purity of his soul," came the answer. This reply reflected the philosophical view that the purpose of humanity is self-perfection and that moral commandments are part of a practical program of spiritual discipline. The Kotzker, however, rejected this approach and responded in anger, "Yankl, is that what we learned from the Holy Yehudi? Rather man was created to lift up the heavens." Lifting up the heavens entails creating a holy life and elevating that life up to the divine itself. Human beings must fashion a spiritual world and then establish it as a model of purity and holiness. When the Kotzker practiced Jewish religion he did so as an active participant in the divine process of sanctifying the world; he was taking the holy from human life and raising it up as a divine ideal. Although human beings exist in the material world, their task lies beyond that world. They must create spirit out of matter and then exalt the spirit that they have conceived.[28] This radicalism suggests that Jews challenge assumptions about their religious world view, to the extent of trying to teach religion even to God.

Rubenstein may criticize the Jewish world view for not accepting the facts of existence. The radical revolution of the Kotzker, however, suggests that covenantal obligation entails revision of religion. To fulfill the duty of affirming personal identity, of maintaining Jewish uniqueness, Jews like the Kotzker may be expected to transform the tradition.

The Kotzker's renovation of Judaism also renewed covenantal perspectives on community. He was known to lament that had he found only the requisite disciples, and performed certain basic spiritual exercises, then his purpose would have been accomplished. Because the Hasidic world of his time lacked such disciples, the Kotzker failed to create a new communal life.

Rubenstein might use the Kotzker as an example of another political paradigm that did not work, of a failed covenantal experiment. Menahem Mendel, in contrast, focused his attention on the goal, revitalizing community, rather than on whether he accomplished it. The act of striving itself — the urge for renewal — was more important than success or failure. The Kotzker's aim, however, mirrors that of the modern Jew. Modernity requires a new definition of covenantal community, its obligations, expectations, and above all its relationship to God. That final concern represents the most radical aspect of the Kotzker's revolution. He demanded that his followers reconceive the nature of the divine and its expectations of humanity. He rejected an identification of the divine will with the details of specifically Judaic laws. He argued, using the phrase attributed to Moses in Deuteronomy 10:12, that God required what Moses had demanded, "only to fear God," and sought to show selected disciples the "small paths" they could take to attain that goal. Unfortunately the few who followed him did not achieve what he had hoped for them.[29] This ecumenical perspective might satisfy even Richard Rubenstein; it certainly appealed to Abraham Heschel, influencing him to present the Kotzker and Kierkegaard in tandem. The Kotzker did not emphasize the parochial, isolating elements of Jewish tradition but sought to find ways to religion that might be more accessible to those who followed independent impulses. Modern Jews may well seek those "small paths" that may represent a more ecumenical journey than that taken by the "great path" of traditional Judaism.

The Kotzker emphasized innovation, change, and progress, insisting, as Abraham Heschel puts it, that "one cannot truly sing by repeating an old melody . . . one must sing a new song each time."[30] The Kotzker guides modern Jews as they attempt to sing new covenant melodies before God, expressing personal identity, communal organization, and inclusive religious living and religious symbols.

NOTES

1.   See Dov Katz, *The Musar Movement*, Vol. 4 (Tel Aviv: Reem, 1978), p. 200–201.

2.   Will Herberg, *Judaism and Modern Man: An Interpretation of Jewish Religion* (New York: Harper and Row, 1951), p. 34.

3.   See Meir Urian, *In the Circle of Hasidism and in the Paths of Our Times* [Hebrew] (Jerusalem: Rubin Mass, 1977), p. 65; see the discussion on modern society in contrast to Hasidic community on pp. 62–64 as well.

4.   Ibid., p. 45.

5.   Raphael Jospe, "Jewish Particularity From Ha-Levi to Kaplan," *Forum* 46/47 (1982), p. 87; see the entire essay, pp. 77–90, for a good discussion of the distinction between an essentialist and formalist definition of Jewishness.

6.   See the discussion in Norman Linzer, *The Nature of Man in Judaism and Social Work* (New York: Commission on Synagogue Relations, 1978), pp. 136–61.

7.   Milton M. Gordon, "Marginality and the Jewish Intellectual," in *The Ghetto and Beyond: Essays on Jewish Life in America*, ed. Peter I. Rose (New York: Random House, 1969), p. 489; see the entire essay, pp. 477–91.

8.   Jacob Neusner, *The Jewish War Against the Jews: Reflections on Golah, Shoah, and Torah* (New York: Ktav, 1984), p. 115.

9.   Eliezer Berkovits, *Faith After the Holocaust* (New York: Ktav, 1973), p. 69.

10.   See Martin Buber, *A Land of Two Peoples: Martin Buber on Jews and Arabs*, ed. with commentary by Paul R. Mendes-Flohr (New York: Oxford University Press, 1983), p. 143.

11.   Jacob Bernard Agus, *Dialogue and Tradition: The Challenges of Contemporary Judeo-Christian Thought* (New York: Abelard-Schuman, 1971), p. 376.

12.   See Hayim Halevy Donin, *To Be a Jew: A Guide to Jewish Observance in Contemporary Life* (New York: Basic Books, 1972), p. 34; see the discussion on pp. 34–38, in which he raises the challenge of assimilation in conjunction with the universal Jewish task.

13.   Agus, *Dialogue and Tradition*, p. 65; see his general discussion in the various essays on interfaith dialogue in part I of this book.

14.   Richard L. Rubenstein, "The Meaning of Torah in Contemporary Jewish Theology," and "The Rebirth of Israel in Contemporary Jewish Theology," in *After Auschwitz: Biblical Theology and Contemporary Judaism* (New York: Bobbs-Merrill, 1966), pp. 112–42, but note his reservations on p. 130.

15.   Ibid., p. 119.

16.   Ibid., p. 188. Cohen's later work takes this critique seriously; see *If*

Not Now, When?: Toward a Reconstruction of the Jewish People, Conversations Between Mordecai Kaplan and Arthur A. Cohen (New York: Schocken, 1973).

17. Ibid., p. 154.

18. Rubenstein, "Religion and History: Power, History and the Covenant at Sinai," in Jacob Neusner, ed., *Take Judaism, for Example: Studies Toward the Comparison of Religions* (Chicago: University of Chicago Press, 1983), pp. 165–83.

19. Ibid., pp. 165, 176.

20. See Rubenstein, *The Cunning of History: The Holocaust and the American Future* (New York: Harper and Row, 1978).

21. See Michael Berenbaum, *The Vision of the Void: Theological Reflections on the Works of Elie Wiesel* (Middletown, Conn.: Wesleyan University Press, 1979), pp. 160–71.

22. Rubenstein, *After Auschwitz*, pp. 80–81.

23. Rubenstein, *Cunning of History*, p. 6.

24. See Rubenstein, *The Age of Triage: Fear and Hope in an Overcrowded World* (Boston: Beacon Press, 1983).

25. Ibid., pp. 232–38.

26. Ibid., p. 240.

27. See Menahem Mendel of Kotzk, *Emet ve Emunah*, 3rd rev. ed. (Jerusalem: 1972); Abraham Joshua Heschel, *A Passion for Truth* (New York: Farrar, Straus and Giroux, 1973); Martin Buber, *Tales of the Hasidim: Later Masters*, trans. Olga Marx (New York: Schocken, 1961), pp. 39–44; Elie Wiesel, *Souls on Fire* (New York: Random House, 1972), pp. 228–54.

28. Mendel, *Emet ve Emunah*, p. 109.

29. Ibid., p. 7.

30. Heschel, *Passion for Truth*, p. 284.

3

Covenant and Personal Identity

PERSONAL COVENANT IN AN AGE OF AUSCHWITZ

The Kotzker Rebbe, as noted in the previous chapter, offered a way of reconceiving Jewish religion appropriate for contemporary Jews. The modern Jew who accepts covenantal obligations wonders how these obligations create a sphere of partnership between the divine and the human. The Kotzker emphasized that God needs humanity even more than human beings need God. The purpose for which God created humanity, he thought, was the exalting of heaven, the lifting up of ideals. God requires the vision and activism of humanity to improve the world.

Elie Wiesel emphasizes this aspect of the Kotzker. He portrays Rabbi Menahem Mendel as a warrior fighting the battles of faith and dreams. The rebbe seeks to change the world, but his fight is both absurd and impossible. Wiesel pictures the Kotzker early in his career ready to storm heaven. He seeks "some companions" and struggles to go not to the woods but "to climb the roof of the universe carrying sauerkraut and straw." Once there, the rebbe shouts that God is God and thus achieves a certain type of victory. A victory precisely because it affirms meaning in the midst of absurdity.[1]

Covenantal theology, on this account, understands God as the source of human yearning, as the goal of human striving. The Kotzker in this version is an absurd hero teaching his disciples to think about themselves and their world in unconventional ways. He rejects the distinction often drawn between the mundane and the supernal, between common sense and religious ideas. He brings up to heaven the most ordinary of things — food fit for commoners and the bedding upon which the poor must lie. The Kotzker's realism, his insistence upon exalting the everyday, receives an ironic twist in this retelling. The statement that "God is God" must be proclaimed not on earth, not to all Jews, but to the heavens themselves. The Kotzker represents an absurdist view of reality, a world view of inclusive scope that leads Jews to confront the facticity not only of their own lives but of all human existence and to transform that facticity and improve it.

An often cited story reflects the peculiar challenge that his view of the Jewish task entails. The Kotzker, according to this tale, once demanded of his disciples, "Where is God?" When they remained silent he answered the question himself — God is wherever a human being allows divinity to enter.[2] The major task faced by contemporary Jews, on this reading, becomes that of preparing an entrance for divinity into human life. Covenantal obedience, as it pertains to individual actions, requires continuous struggle to use commonplace routine as an antechamber to divinity.

Many Jews fail in this struggle. Abraham Joshua Heschel sensed this failure when he charged that contemporary Jews capitulate to indifference, lamenting that "our cardinal sin is that we do not grasp the sublime in our existence, that we do not know how to adjust our lives to the grandeur, our thoughts to the mystery."[3] Modern Jews do fall prey to despair, remain insensitive to the sublime within ordinary existence, and adjust themselves to vulgar culture rather than to grandeur. The Kotzker teaches that covenantal imperatives challenge Jews to change their lives and to discover meaning in a chaotic world.

Covenantal obligation includes more than the duty to confront the facticity of the world. Judaism demands that Jews see both themselves and cosmos filled with meaning and to recognize that God enters the world not only through nature but, more specifically, through human nature. Human beings, Heschel declares, search "for significant being."[4] Covenant duty takes this search seriously. Covenant obligation demands that Jews actualize freedom and "choose life." Declaring the duty for freedom also affirms its possibility; yet many modern Jews fall prey to despair—they consider their lives hedged in with conditions that determine their existence, they deny their ability to make choices. Will Herberg identifies such despair as "idolatry." When Jews reject freedom, according to this view, they abandon covenant obligation, they become enslaved to other creatures, and thereby, they deny the reality of the creator.[5] Fidelity to covenant meaning implies living as if freedom were the ultimate truth and rejecting determinism.

The primary covenantal directive obligates Jews to rise above the facticity of modernity and to stand against pessimistic analyses of individual potential. Can Jews do so responsibly, without falling into fantasy or wishful thinking? The expectations that correspond to these obligations of the individual Jew focus on an actualization of human potential. To obey God means to become more fully human. At the heart of that assertion lies another claim: human beings are most truly themselves when they surpass mere humanity and become like God. Covenant, ultimately, promises the individual a chance to imitate the deity: "You shall be holy as I the Lord your God am holy" (Leviticus 19:2). This commandment suggests that covenantal obedience creates a humanistic world community in which, by imitating God, every human being treats every other human being with love, respect, and neighborliness (Mekhilta, Shirata Chapter 3). While Jews begin covenantal living by affirming their personal identity, they eventually discover that the meaning of being a self leads to an improved human community.

Such a paradigm seems strangely unrealistic in a modern world that has experienced Auschwitz and Hiroshima. Humanity appears more capable of destroying meaning than of creating it. Assurances that fulfillment of covenantal obligations heightens awareness of personal meaning and personal significance seem disconfirmed by the facts of modernity. The psychological discomfort arising from the conflicting claims of tradition and experience has been studied by sociologists, who call such a phenomenon "cognitive dissonance." The idea, at its most stark, suggests that when faced with evidence disconfirming deeply felt beliefs, human beings are often plunged into confusion. They seek strategies for reconciling the challenged beliefs with the evidence at hand. The concept itself, while enjoying some sociological renown, may well be criticized as limited and simplistic.[6] It does, however, raise questions about the ethical expectations of covenantal religion. Jewish thinkers defend human freedom, potential for good, and the possibility that through obedience to covenantal obligation human beings may find personal self-actualization. Such contentions, however, may be the result of self-deception and may merely illustrate a natural response to psychological discomfort. Jewish responses to the disconfirmation of their covenantal expectations may be explained as a natural way of coping with disappointment. Perhaps these ways of reducing cognitive dissonance merely represent a tactic of self-deception. A defense of covenantal religion as it applies to contemporary Jews must not only demonstrate how ordinary life may be perceived as a vehicle for the sublime or how obedience to covenantal laws reinforces a sense of personal significance, but also how such perceptions of the sublime and of individual worth represent more than merely wishful thinking. Strangely enough, a confrontation with the lessons of the Nazi holocaust suggests that covenantal expectations may not be unrealistic or self-deceivng.

COVENANT AND WORLD VIEW IN THE
PERSPECTIVE OF THE HOLOCAUST

Covenant obligation insists that Jews affirm meaning in the universe. God's reality becomes clear through the struggle to discern significance in history. Some modern Jews argue the absurdity of trying to find historical meaning in a world that made Auschwitz possible. Others, however, use the evidence of the holocaust to affirm human meaning.

Students of the holocaust note that survivors often displayed a clear sense of purpose, a transcendent goal, and a definite belief in life's meaning. Viktor Frankl and Terence Des Pres have concluded that those who discover meaning in their lives are more likely to survive tribulations and privations. Thus Des Pres, focusing his studies on individual survivors, finds that they possess a sense of their connection with other people because they have created an imaginative community with whom they identify. These are the type of people whom Des Pres characterizes as taking "intelligent action to make explicit and effective" the interrelationship of personal identity and community.[7]

Community plays an essential covenantal role. Individual identity may be a personal discovery, a private realization. Covenant obligation, however, moves beyond interior life. To obey covenant duties means to make a public gesture, even if that gesture affirms a personal sense of life's significance. The first personal duty of the Jew who takes covenant seriously entails communication with this imaginative community, indicating through explicit gestures a sense of connection not only within personal life but between the life of the individual and the reality outside of the individual. Lawrence Langer expresses this sense of obligation, this first covenantal duty, and generalizes it. He suggests that human beings generally need to communicate their view of reality, their construction of existence, to a group of others. He claims that "men seek a gesture to affirm the human in the midst of threatened chaos."[8] These gestures may be understood as testimony that the mean-

ing asserted and the expectations fulfilled point beyond themselves. Human beings communicate to others the "good news"
that the ability to affirm meaning in the midst of chaos shows
a more than human presence pervading reality.

Such a vision of the world might seem unrealistic. The
impetus to such covenant observance, however, is rooted in
human nature. Realists such as Rubenstein, it could be argued,
have ignored an important fact about humanity. Human beings
are symbol-making creatures. To be human means to intuit or
to establish significance in reality as well as to experience it.
Such thinkers, some Jewish theologians contend, underes-
timate "the source and staying power of covenantal theism." A
theory of human living that ignores the vital role that human
consciousness plays, that overlooks the way in which individuals shape reality by evaluating it, cannot claim to be
based on an unbiased analysis of the facticity of existence.
Modern history teaches that human beings are more than just
"fact-finding animals" but are also "value-hungry." Interpreted
in this way, covenant obligation entails accepting the inevitable, recognizing one's internal reality, the facticity of the
human being's need for a story that explains reality. In this way,
the covenant duty to affirm meaning in the face of absurdity
reflects a coming to terms with the very nature of human
existence.[9]

AFFIRMING THE MEANING OF THE WORLD

The nature of the obligation, expectations, and sense of
divinity found in this natural response to experience pervades
Jewish tradition. At times Jews have interpreted history as a
divine narrative — human events represent the script in which
God writes a divine autobiography. At other times history
appears as an anthropological self-portrait depicting the glory
and shame of human beings — suffering as punishment stands
for human sinfulness, triumph as reward for obedience, "chas-
tisements accepted out of love" as metaphors for holiness.

Above all, Jewish thought emphasizes the almost arrogant affirmation that human beings impose meaning and significance on experience.

A medieval tale, brought by the historian Solomon Ibn Verga in his attempt to comprehend the history of Spanish Jewry — its rise to success and prosperity, its decline, and its final suffering and expulsion — expresses this covenantal self-affirmation. In 1492, when Spain exiled all its Jewish citizens, Jewish thinkers began to reevaluate their traditional views of covenant in similar ways to those of theologians today in the wake of the Nazi experience. Ibn Verga portrays Jewish sufferings from the earliest postbiblical times through the experiences of the Spanish refugees. This pastiche of ancient sources is presented as a coherent tale of Jewish suffering throughout history and offers an explanation of them. One tale tells how, despite bitter experience, one of the Jewish exiles from Spain affirmed his belief.[10] He had fled Spain with his wife and children on a plague-infested ship. His wife died on board, the ship was wrecked, and after carrying his children, he fell faint; upon awakening he discovered that they had died. Out of his sorrow he cried to God. His cry, however, demonstrated commitment to covenantal duty, not despair:

> Master of the Universe, You have done much so that I would abandon my religion. Yet I am still a Jew and a Jew I shall remain. Neither that which you have brought upon me nor that which you still may bring upon me will be of any avail.

An often neglected epilogue to the tale reports that the father buried his children and sought to find the Jews with whom he had traveled. He could not find them, however, since "the company of Jews had not waited lest they die as well. Thus each was concerned with his own sorrow and gave no attention to that of his fellow." Yet despite this reality, Ibn Verga's hero contends that God must be affirmed. He despairs of every human basis for hope and belief — trust in history, in being able to help family and loved ones, in being able to trust in a community of others. Despite this experience, because of it, the hero cries out to the "master of the universe" and demonstrates through what he does the presence of the divine.

This heroic self-identification as a Jew imposes three types of signification on reality. Ibn Verga's hero refuses to acknowledge a lack of purpose but understands suffering as trial and testing. Confronting the meaninglessness of family ties, the hero maintains a humanity, a loving care. Finally, despite the callous and uncaring attitude of other Jews, the hero affirms the reality of Jewish community. The author may add an ironic footnote—Jews act like beasts to one another, but the hero acts as if a caring communal order still existed. The story reflects not only how human beings create meaning and how they impose that meaning on life but also that this significance can be imposed on God, as a metaphor for cosmic order and value.

SELFHOOD AND MEANING AS COVENANTAL OBLIGATION

Ibn Verga's hero announces his decision to remain a Jew out of a clear sense of personal value and worth. Many modern Jews lack just that sense of value. While Abraham Heschel grounds human significance in its transcendent meaning, Ibn Verga's story indicates that at times the reality of transcendent meaning itself needs grounding. Suffering may undermine more than belief in life's value; it may destroy self-confidence as well. Covenantal obligation includes the duty of affirming personal significance, to confirm the value of being an independent self. Without confidence in one's own worth, a person lacks the strength and ability to impose meaning on the outside world. Sometimes, however, covenant theology itself appears to attack self-confidence. When the prophets declared God's destruction of Israel justified because of Jewish sinfulness, they launched an attack on Jewish self-understanding. Blaming the victim for being victimized may slowly sap away initiative and motivation for meaning-affirming actions. Self-disgust makes performing gestures of significance difficult.

In response to this possibility Jewish tradition has again and again rewritten history. The rabbinic interpreters of the Bible have often reprimanded the prophets because they dared to cast aspersions on the Jewish people who "if they are not prophets are at least the heirs of the prophets." While theological biographies of a sinful people justify divine justice, rabbinic writers claim that prophets should justify the people of Israel. The theology of the rabbis often castigates sinners while exonerating the average Jew. When a theology of history has seemed to impugn Jewish self-respect, the rabbis have reconceived Jewish thought to restore each Jew's personal esteem.[11] Tales of Jewish heroism and theological reinterpretations of history present more acceptable images of Jewish identity. The rabbis replace sinful biography with more respectable stories; they employ "biographic rehabilitation."[12] In the face of an untenable history, a "sinful" biography, Jews reconstruct the past in ways more conducive to survival. When human beings define themselves in a new way, they also redefine the reality they encounter as a challenge to reconceive the meaning of covenantal duty.

The Nazi holocaust requires a biographic rehabilitation similar to that of earlier Jewish times. Survivors of that event find diverse ways of coping with their experience. They feel pain at the losses they have sustained; they know guilt because of surviving when others have perished; they express anger at a creator who subjects creations to such torture. These reactions need rehabilitation. Elie Wiesel focuses on these challenges to selfhood. His heroes face extreme situations: they must make choices between life and death, silence and screaming, piety and impiety, murder and indifference. Throughout his narratives, however, Wiesel maintains a thematic unity. He justifies human anger, he legitimates expressions of pain, he rehabilitates survivors who hardly recognize what they have become. A note of protest against the deity runs through his writing as a leitmotif. He locates within the covenantal paradigm the right to challenge the divine – "the privilege of judging God."[13] This response to the holocaust insists that the human part of the divine covenant implies utilizing the inevitable experiences of life, including experiences of pain and suffering, to develop a unique selfhood even in conflict with the divine. Even God's honor must be set aside for the sake of Jewish self-respect.

The covenantal obligation of affirming the value of each individual, then, entails protest no less than affirmation, rejecting philosophies that suggest unalterable guilt or sinfulness. The protest that arises from such an approach constitutes its own reward. By fighting against the imperfect, Jews discover that the world may be perfected, that nature is not yet fully realized, that human beings contribute to an ongoing process of cosmic improvement.

Sometimes the challenge for improvement occurs within the individual and implies a struggle against internal obstacles rather than a protest even against the deity. Biographic rehabilitation may entail reconstructing one's inner self, one's passions and impulses. The Musar Movement, discussed earlier in relation to Rabbi Yossel Horwitz, represents just that midrashic rehabilitation of biography necessary in the modern world. The life and teachings of Rabbi Israel Salanter, the founder of the Musar Movement, provide a perspective on how struggling to rehabilitate an individual's sense of self and personhood leads to a sense of divinity in the world.[14] Salanter recognized the problematic nature of the human self: each person faces a sea of passion threatening to overwhelm the intellect. He recognized that covenant impels Jews to transform the imperfect, to protest against the less than fully realized. Desire forms a river in which a person would sink were it not for the boat of spiritual feelings.[15] From this standpoint the Torah, Jewish law and teachings, provide an antidote that enables each Jew to achieve self-improvement. Each person's struggle with the evil inclination leads to discovering self-worth.

Modern Jews, like those at the time of Salanter, recognize their internal turmoil. They seek to cope with competing emotions, overpowering passions. By seeing their struggle as part of a covenantal duty, these Jews learn that they are not alone. Their internal battle represents a genuinely human activity; not only do they gain personal satisfaction from a victory over their untempered impulses, but they fulfill an obligation that promises to make their lives more significant.

This view suggests the transcendent meaning of personal struggle. The world as a whole benefits when Jews triumph over their chaotic passions. Contemporary Jews can learn to take the opening chapters of Genesis seriously. The first chapter presents a blueprint of perfection and an imperative that humanity act as a divine vice-regent in administrating the creation of that perfection. The second chapter, however, begins by picturing a dry and barren land, unproductive because no man tills the soil. Nature, this story seems to imply, requires human cultivation in order to flourish. Only when each human being reaches full potential will the world reach its potential as well. Salanter expressed this idea as an allegory: as rain depends on mist for its life-giving force, so God depends on drawing up power from humanity.[16] God's role in human development seems to come from the responsiveness inherent in the natural order. The symbiosis between humanity and an imperfect world — symbolized by each person's inner struggle — reveals a pattern in reality. To be fully human means to struggle against imperfection, to anticipate self-improvement, and to experience the responsiveness of nature. Such an experience affirms the value of each individual's deeds, not just as a process of self-perfection but also as part of the perfection of the world.

FREEDOM OF THE WILL AND COVENANTAL OBLIGATION

The possibility of affirming either cosmic meaning or personal worth depends upon an assumption that human beings freely choose to act — either in evaluating the world or in defining the shape of their lives. Covenantal obligation, as already noted, requires imposing significance on the chaos of existence and following the specific injunctions of Torah in a private struggle to conquer internal passions. Neither of these events has ultimate purpose if it represents the inevitable responses of human beings to uncontrollable conditions that in fact constrain their actions. Traditionally, of course, such freedom is a given; to deny freedom means to deny God. In Herberg's terms it means to accept the dictates of an "idol." Faced with impotence both internally and externally, however, many Jews find the temptation to such idolatry overwhelming.

During the Nazi holocaust, Jews experienced the degradation of being transformed into victims. Many Jews responded with heroism; Jewish partisans and ghetto uprisings testify to the strength many Jews discovered within themselves in the face of overwhelming odds. The direct assault of the Nazis on Jewish self-esteem, however, has been augmented by an indirect assault by the social sciences. Modern Jews have been taught to "suspect yourself as you suspect your neighbor." Psychology strips away the mask of politeness and refinement to reveal the naked human beast. Sociologists discover how the pressure for conformity and the dynamics of social movements undermine personal initiative and independence. Contemporary Jews may desire to affirm the obligations of covenant but may also feel that they have no real option. Those who obey do so out of constraint; those who disobey do so from equally compelling conditioning. Under such circumstances, praising those who follow the covenant makes no more sense than criticizing those who fail to fulfill its obligations. As Irving Greenberg suggests, Jews today need to revive "the sense of option and choice" that modern experience has undermined.[17]

Covenantal theology demands some understanding of human choice that may still be affirmed in the modern period. The argument for free will traditionally occurs in relation to the problem of theodicy. An all-powerful deity, it might be thought, would create a world without evil. Either God lacks the power to create perfection or the will to benefit the creatures. God's gift of free will provides a solution to this dilemma. God, so the argument runs, created a beneficent world. Human beings were blessed with freedom of the will as a special dispensation. God limits divine providence to preserve that blessing and interferes in human life without hindering human freedom.[18] Modern Jews, however, frame the question in a more anthropological way. They do not ask how a good God could allow evil but rather how human beings may be expected to respond creatively given experienced determinism.

The traditional view of free will, however, does offer some suggestive indications of how modern Jews might affirm the reality of free will. Traditionally, God's providence extends to all areas of life except attitude. Thus the Mishna states, "All is foreseen but free will is given," even though the midrash declares, "Even before a thought is framed in a man's heart, it is already known to God." On the other hand, citing Deuteronomy 10:12, Rav Hanina declared that everything is in the hands of God except the fear of heaven.[19] This latter emphasizes that human beings' contributions to the divine reside in the attitudes they display rather than in particular deeds, which may or may not be beneficial to the world.

This traditional approach recognizes life's inevitable structure but sees it as the framework within which each person evolves a world view, an attitude toward reality. The element of surprise and spontaneity lies within each person's consciousness, not in the unexpectedness of external events but in the unpredictability of human attitudes. Perhaps the most important aspect of this approach lies in its recognition that human beings can be constantly surprised by themselves, by others, and by the reaction of the world. Human knowledge is so limited that while the macro-forces of the world may indeed determine all actions, the individual as a personal microcosm may respond to that determined structure with surprise, with apparent unpredictability and inner astonishment.[20]

This covenantal obligation, this demand for responsive spontaneity, reflects freedom of attitude. Under covenant duties, Jews allow themselves to be surprised, permit themselves astonishment at the world and at themselves. Covenant demands a certain attitudinal stance – a willingness to look for the unexpected. Beyond that willingness, convenant obliges recognition of the need for others. Becoming a self depends upon relationship to the non-self. Not only does a Jew become self-aware by sharing an imaginative community of meaning and by affirming personal worth, the final assurance of individual value comes from other people, from recognizing the interactive nature of human importance.

Maurice Friedman recognizes this aspect of human development. He contends that "you cannot know who you are if you have not let yourself come forth in response to a call greater than yourself."[21] The paradox in this statement is that an individual becomes free, develops as a true self, by accepting the pressure of an outside other. Free will from this perspective refers to a willing acceptance of others, an openness to precisely those others in the human environment that shape and mold the self. The attitude that the tradition considers one of "freedom" proclaims the inevitability of interacting with the "operant conditioners" in the environment. According to this view, human beings become unique individuals through dialogue with others because, as Friedman suggests, "Dialogue . . . confirms the other yet does not deny oneself . . . [it] is at once a confirmation of community and of otherness."[22] The possibility of dialogue seems natural and may be taken for granted. A theological understanding of the mystery of human mutuality, the strange reality that occurs between people, indicates that more may be at stake than the determinism of social and natural forces. Martin Buber, for example, recognizes that God can be known not only through the two expressions of matter and form, but also in a third mode – that of personhood. God as person ensures the possibility of human meeting.

This understanding of God's role as guarantor of the "between," of the possibility of mutuality, allows for freedom. Human beings are free because they do not exist as "monads," as isolate entities. The possibility of human interaction reveals a depth dimension to human experience. Freedom, defined as the possibility of being surprised by others and by oneself, occurs because meeting with the non-self remains a real option. The divine may well be identified, as for example Martin Buber identified it, with the ground of such meeting and encounter. Indeed, Buber considers the independence that God gives to humanity just this power of spontaneous dialogue and surprise.[23]

Survivors of the holocaust, those who might well consider themselves the ultimate victims, sometimes testify to the reality of this type of freedom. They do not deny a type of compulsion acting upon them. They do, however, interpret that compulsion in a spirit of freedom, as evidence that they too can find surprise through their relationships with others. A Hasidic tale born from the holocaust tells how Yoav Kimmelman abandoned Jewish tradition after his liberation from the death camps. Finding no rationale for Jewish religious life unrefuted by the holocaust, he rejected every precept of tradition. Once, however, he was induced to join a group at worship in order to fill out the required number for a prayer quorum. When forced by circumstances to read from the Torah scroll for the sake of others, he did so. At that point, he recounts, the letters of the Torah reached out to him. He gives no rational explanation for his return to tradition; he blames his renewed Jewishness on the inherent power of the Hebrew letters themselves.[24] The power of the letters surprised him. By responding to the others in his environment, Yoav Kimmelman discovered aspects of his own identity that he had not suspected. By fulfilling the covenantal obligation of openness, by his willingness to expect the unexpected, he experienced the fulfillment of his expectations. In that fulfillment he saw and testified concerning a power and presence that defied reason, that could be described as the effects of divinity on his life.

COVENANTAL ETHICS

This first view of covenant, covenant as an agreement between individuals and God, focuses on personal obligations. Individuals must affirm cosmic meaning, personal worth, and the value of others in expectation that they will discover coherence in life, their own personal value, and a world capable of surprising them. These three rewards combine to reinforce a sense of wonder at the world, an intimation of divinity. Taken by itself, however, this covenantal perspective seems selfish and overly introspective. Jews face a danger, inherent in this type of covenantal emphasis, of limiting themselves to a narrow perspective, as some scholars analyzing the holocaust recognize. Thus George Kren warns that the proper response to the holocaust must be the "affirmation of the universality of human rights."[25] Performance of covenantal duties applicable to individuals must lead into more social and communal concerns. Such a warning, however, may be unnecessary. Personal covenant represents a point of departure, not a conclusion of the human quest. Covenantal obligation begins by focusing on the private life of every individual Jew. Once individual Jews discover their personal duties, however, they also learn that they are inherently linked with other Jews in a community of concern. Private religious experience points beyond itself. William James intimates that those who find personal meaning in their lives are "inspired to exemplary community service, and moral rectitude."[26] Judaism defines the nature of community service and moral rectitude in covenantal terms no less than it defines personal covenant in those terms. The following chapter explores these duties as appropriate and compelling for contemporary Jews.

NOTES

1. Elie Wiesel, *Souls on Fire* (New York: Random House, 1972), p. 243.
2. See Abraham Joshua Heschel, *A Passion for Truth* (New York:

Farrar, Straus and Giroux, 1973), p. 33; Martin Buber, *Hasidism and Modern Man*, ed. and trans. Maurice Friedman (New York: Horizon Press, 1958), pp. 34–35; Wiesel, *Souls on Fire*, p. 248.

3.   Heschel, *The Insecurity of Freedom: Essays on Human Existence* (New York: Schocken, 1972), p. 189; Heschel, *Who Is Man?* (Stanford: Stanford University Press, 1965), p. 116.

4.   Heschel, *Who Is Man?*, p. 51; see the argument throughout the book.

5.   Will Herberg, *Judaism and Modern Man: An Interpretation of Jewish Religion* (New York: Harper and Row, 1951), pp. 92–102.

6.   See Leon Festinger, *The Theory of Cognitive Dissonance* (Evanston: Row, Peterson, 1957); compare Jonathan Z. Smith, "No Need to Travel to the Indies: Judaism and the Study of Religion," in Jacob Neusner, ed., *Take Judaism, for Example: Studies Toward the Comparison of Religions* (Chicago: University of Chicago Press, 1983), pp. 222–24.

7.   Terence Des Pres, *Survivor: An Anatomy of Life in the Death Camps* (New York: Pocket Books, 1977), p. 13; compare Viktor E. Frankl, *Man's Search for Meaning: An Introduction to Logotherapy* (Boston: Beacon Press, 1959).

8.   Lawrence Langer, "The Divided Voice: Elie Wiesel and the Challenge of the Holocaust," in *Confronting the Holocaust: The Impact of Elie Wiesel*, ed. Alvin H. Rosenfeld and Irving Greenberg (Bloomington: Indiana University Press, 1978), p. 41.

9.   David Hartman, *A Living Covenant: The Innovative Spirit in Traditional Judaism* (New York: The Free Press, 1985), p. 203.

10.   Solomon Ibn Verga, *Shevet Yehuda* (Tel Aviv: Schocken, 1946), p. 125; Nahum N. Glatzer, ed., *A Jewish Reader: In Time and Eternity* (New York: Schocken, 1961), pp. 204–5.

11.   See Nahum N. Glatzer, "A Study of the Talmudic-Midrashic Interpretation of Prophecy," in *Essays in Jewish Thought* (University, Alabama: University of Alabama Press, 1978), pp. 16–35.

12.   See Mordechai Rotenberg, "The 'Midrash' and Biographic Rehabilitation," *Journal for the Scientific Study of Religion* 25 (1986), pp. 41–55.

13.   Byron L. Sherwin, "Wiesel's Midrash," in Rosenfeld and Greenberg, *Confronting the Holocaust*, p. 124.

14.   See Hillel Goldberg, *Israel Salanter, Text, Structure, and Idea: The Ethics and Theology of an Early Psychologist of the Unconscious* (New York: Ktav, 1982); see also Dov Katz, *The Musar Movement*, Vol. 1 (Tel Aviv: Reem, 1978); and for primary texts, Mordecai Pachter, *Israel Salanter: Selected Writings* [in Hebrew] (Jerusalem: Bialik Institute, 1972).

15.   See Pachter, *Israel Salanter*, p. 114.

16.   Ibid., pp. 93, 189.

17.   Irving Greenberg, "Clouds of Smoke, Pillar of Fire: Judaism, Christianity, and Modernity After the Holocaust," in *Auschwitz: Beginning of a New Era? Reflections on the Holocaust*, ed. Eva Fleschner (New York: Ktav, 1977), pp. 7–55; see especially pp. 50–52.

18.   See Emil L. Fackenheim, "Human Freedom and Divine Power," in *Quest for Past and Future: Essays in Jewish Theology* (Bloomington: Indiana University Press, 1968), pp. 338–43; see Kenneth R. Seeskin, "The Reality of Radical Evil," *Judaism* 19:4 (1980), pp. 450–53.

19.   See Avot 3:19; Genesis Rabba, Genesis 9:3; Berachot 33b.

20.   For a summary of various traditional defenses of the idea of free will see Joseph Grunblatt, "Freedom of the Will: A Traditionalist's View," *Tradition* 10:4 (1969), pp. 48–59; compare this with the argument in Shubert Spero, *Morality, Halakha, and the Jewish Tradition* (New York: Ktav, 1983), pp. 236–73, and Avrohom Worob, "The Free-Will Determinism Issue," in *Duties of the Mind: Essays on Jewish Philosophy*, ed. Nova Worob (Spring Valley: Shaare Emet, 1975), pp. 44–46.

21.   Maurice Friedman, *The Hidden Human Image* (New York: Dell, 1974), p. 255.

22.   Ibid., p. 369.

23.   Martin Buber, *The Eclipse of God: Studies in the Relation Between Religion and Philosophy*, trans. Maurice Friedman (New York: Harper and Brothers, 1952), p. 138.

24.   See Yaffa Eliach, *Hasidic Tales of the Holocaust* (New York: Oxford University Press, 1982), pp. 202–4.

25.   George M. Kren, "The Holocaust: Some Unresolved Issues," in *Annals of Scholarship*, Vol. 3 (1984), p. 49.

26.   William James, *The Varieties of Religious Experience*, ed. Martin E. Marty (New York: Penguin Books, 1982), pp. 369–70.

4

Covenant and Jewish Community

COMMUNAL OBLIGATIONS UNDER COVENANT

Covenant consists of an agreement between an individual and the divine; it may also consist of an agreement with a collectivity, a community. Covenantal community in this latter sense extends the boundaries of obligation, expectation, and the divine presence to include social organization and political behavior. The obligations devolving on individuals, expectations for self-realization, and sensitivity to the divine ground of personal life point outward to community. The major obligation placed upon such communal covenant observance consists of constructing a social order responsive to the needs of its members. Fulfillment of this obligation promises to achieve the ideals and values for which individuals come together to create community. The variety of communal strategies effecting the link between obligation and expectation reveals the divine presence.

That connection, however, often appears more theoretical than practical. Minority groups, in particular, feel the oppressive rather than liberating effects of political institutions. Leadership often represses those whom it should foster and protect. The desire for social expediency often obscures God's presence in society. Jewish leadership has sometimes conceived of traditional social law, of *halakha*, as an end in itself rather than as a means to the formation of responsive community. Moses sometimes appears as a dictator and tyrant rather than as an instrument of divine compassion.

Martin Buber understands the problems that can arise within traditional Jewish leadership. He resists the temptation to identify the birth of true community with a mere change of institutions. He rejects the idea that community could be "wrested in common" from a "a resisting world." Instead he claims that community occurs "where community happens" and only takes shape when institutions reflect a reality already present—that of human beings sharing common goals and concerns.[1] According to that philosophy, social morality develops when genuine meeting occurs between human individuals and autonomous others. The only justified communal institutions are those replacing manipulation of others with a cultivation of personal existence and independence by creating a forum for interaction. Obedience to the covenantal obligation of ensuring opportunities for interhuman encounter represents the only possible means of achieving the ideal social or political system.

Buber understands the religious radicalism of the Kotzker Rebbe as an attempt to recall Jewish leadership to its covenantal task. Buber, thus, retells the story of his quest for disciples as a search for true community. According to him, Menahem Mendel would lament that had he but four hundred true followers he would go into the woods with them, give them manna, and show them the kingly power of God.[2] This version stresses the way the Kotzker reveals the basis upon which true community can be built. Community depends on simple living, on removing the barriers of human arrogance established by traditional leadership groups. Leaders who recognize the natural environment (the woods) as the true human habitat will not fall prey to self-aggrandizing building projects. Leaders who acknowledge that nature and God's power limit their authority will not mistake their communal trust for a gift they can use as they wish.

The Kotzker sought, according to Buber, to create natural community. Through establishing a society free from the strategies by which people pretend that they control reality, by which they maintain the fiction that the material world sustains itself, he transforms Jewish institutions so that they serve the community rather than being served by them. Of course, Buber, no less than Wiesel, recognizes that the Kotzker failed; Buber attributes that failure to the times in which he lived, the times of Hasidism's decline. His quest was a good one — the search for authentic communal life. His failure reflects less on him than on the restraints and constraints of traditional Jewish life that could not permit him to succeed. While later Hasidic rebbes bowed to the inevitable, the Kotzker remains a tragic witness both to the nobility of Hasidism's ideals and to their inability to save the Jewish community from spiritual decay.

The pessimism of this story reveals Buber's evaluation of Hasidism as a spiritual resource for contemporary Jews. Buber considers the Kotzker as one of the few "authentic leaders" in the latter part of Hasidism's history. He transforms Rabbi Menahem Mendel into a theological pioneer frustrated by a decaying movement. Buber considers him a transitional figure linking the final glory of Hasidism to the perplexities of modernity. He provided Buber with an example of one rebbe who refused to compromise with the unwillingness of his followers. Buber places the Kotzker during the "twilight of Hasidism" and notes that "we can hear midnight striking," but still considers him a testimony to the power of the movement even in its last moments.[3] The mixed metaphor here should be taken seriously. Buber identifies Menahem Mendel as both the last example of Hasidic ethics and also the death knell to traditional Judaism as such. When the Kotzker failed, so too did traditional Judaism. The ordinary models of Jewish communal life cannot respond to the needs of modern Jews.

THE CIVIL RELIGION OF THE COVENANT

Although traditional Judaism failed, Buber hopes that the example of the Kotzker can illuminate contemporary attempts to establish natural community, to revive Jewish life in the modern world. In this way the "twilight" of Hasidism can point, by its very failure, to possibilities for more contemporary Jewish movements. While the Kotzker never attained his goal, Buber suggests that he did provide a means of reaching it. The Kotzker's advice to his followers offers Buber an alternative to the withdrawal from unnatural society that the story itself demands. Buber draws on the Kotzker's insight into human nature as his most radical achievement. Buber notes three demands made by the Kotzker on his disciples: not to look furtively outside yourself, not to look furtively into others, and not to aim at yourselves.[4] These three directives seem more appropriate for leaders and their policies than for the in-dividual alone. Combined, they define the shape of Jewish communal obligation, of covenant as civil religion.

Civil religion begins as an affirmation of the goals and ideals of a particular people, of a national spirit. As nations and cultures develop they inevitably come into contact with outside influences. They may assimilate these influences and create a new synthesis with them. They may imitate the alien culture without attempting to "naturalize" the borrowings that have been made. The imperative of covenant as civil religion entails a cautious stance towards innovation and change. Those in-novations should maintain the cultural integrity of the nation, should continue the spiritual identity of the group, and should respect the ideals and values for which the community was established.[5]

Understood as civil imperatives, as social directives, Menahem Mendel's advice cautions society and its members as they evolve a sense of their corporate identity. "Do not look furtively outside yourself." This instruction does not entail rejecting all external influence; it does mean recognizing chanes for what they are, and it does demand acknowledgment of change rather than mere tolerance of it. Above all, this imperative demands that a responsive culture consult its members before incorporating foreign elements.

"Do not look furtively into others." Civil religion may become a tyrant rather than an ally to minority groups within a culture. Those who follow divergent paths, whose diversity enriches the cultural potential, whose variety spices national identity, may find their loyalty challenged. When a civil religion looks "furtively" at its dissidents, it undermines the social order. Covenantal obligation entails more than establishing a social order expressive of a particular culture. It demands that minorities be incorporated into that order, that culture itself invite diversity and variety. A civil religion that cultivates exclusivity, that excludes major populations from its sphere of concern, has misunderstood covenantal duty.

"Do not aim at yourself." Buber explicitly connects this saying with religious leadership. While Moses, the authentic Jewish leader, was a humble person "whose doings are not aimed at himself," his archrival, Korah, "took himself" and thereby revealed the inauthenticity of his bid for leadership.[6] Civil religion often becomes the self-legitimation of a particular class. Kings declare themselves divinely authorized; elite groups consider themselves ordained to carry the "burden" of the "disadvantaged." Those who proclaim that they have been divinely destined for certain privileges and programs "aim at themselves." Their ideologies represent civil religion gone awry. Such a civil religion ignores the protests of those whom it oppresses. By aiming at themselves the leaders lose sight of their true mission—providing an environment conducive to personal expression and human interaction for all members of society—and civil religion degenerates into idolatry.

THE OBLIGATIONS AND EXPECTATIONS OF COMMUNAL COVENANT

The Kotzker provides a basis for generating a specific content to covenant as applied to a community. The first obligation concerns the content of a culture. Various paradigms of biblical politics reflect the diverse influences that shaped biblical thought. Covenantal obligation would not deny that cultures mutually affect one another. The covenantal ideal, however, suggests that such manifestations of civil life must be conditioned by the actual needs and concerns of the people. Only when changes occur from within, only when they reflect the true variety of the culture itself, are they legitimate. The ideal judges the effectiveness of each concrete representation. The validity of both the paradigm of democratic covenant (the Exodus story) and that of royal covenant (the covenant with Israel's kings, and especially with King David) depends upon their accurate reflection of the culture they represent. Perhaps Buber intends to refer to this type of test when he declares that a community must allow the individual to enter "into the dialogue of the ages."[7]

Communal organization must fulfill its duty of responding to the reality of its members, but members must also be willing to accept the authority of the group. The relationship between the ruled and the rulers must be reciprocal. The leaders must listen to the voices of the oppressed minorities; both the minorities and the majorities must subordinate their own needs to the authentic needs of the group as a whole. Community as a whole, both the leaders and their followers, faces a difficult task in achieving a balance between private rights and the communal good. The struggle to achieve that balance, however, represents a major duty under covenantal obligations. Buber, for example, recognizes the temptation of "antinomianism," in which the supremacy of the "will of God" becomes an "empty stubbornness which does not wish to bow to any order." This double concern gives specific duties to both the leaders and the general membership in a community.

Leaders must heed the voices of the members; members must respect their leaders' good faith.[8]

Such a dialectic might seem to imply one form of covenantal politics rather than another. The democratic paradigm (Exodus) appears more responsive to the needs of the group than does the royal (Davidic) view of covenant. Nevertheless, Moses sometimes acts as a king and sometimes as a democratic leader. The fault need not lie in the organizational form but in the use to which it is employed. The nation-state, for example, may often create a civil religion that is oppressive even within a democratic community. The important criterion for social responsiveness lies in a willingness to listen to minorities, to hear the protests of those who are oppressed. The presence of such a will to hear tests the sincerity of covenantal community. Whether a community understands its duties to minorities or not may justify its moral position under covenant. Buber himself applies such a test to the State of Israel. He acknowledges its right to exist—without the state no covenantal existence could even be possible. Zionism provides the only opportunity for Jewish covenantal experimentation in the modern world. Yet he challenges Zionists to legitimate their cause by the quality of their interaction with the non-Jewish Arab minority. He demands that the state be sensitive to the Arab problem, since failure to respond adequately to it challenges the state to transform its inner life in order to meet covenantal demands.[9]

COVENANT COMMUNITY AND ITS MINORITIES

The way a Jewish community responds to minority needs provides a touchstone of its civil religion. Does covenant, as a communal ideal, cultivate an inclusive society providing wide access to human relationships? The Hebrew Bible reveals that the people of Israel did not actualize the ideal of a community of equals. Covenantal theory alone could not equalize a mixed group of people. Some members of the community were given tasks and privileges that gave them more status than others.

Some with special status received official sanction – both kings and priests possessed special signs of distinction. The class divisions between rich and poor, farming and business interests, and urban and rural values also created a de facto hierarchy deplored by the theory of a unified community. Sometimes social convention masked the inequalities that hampered human interaction. Class distinctions created a stratified system preventing free encounters between persons.

Despite its covenantal language, the Hebrew Bible manifests an ambivalent attitude towards minorities. References to the Exodus from Egypt emphasize the equal treatment to be given to the stranger, resident alien, and home-born citizen. The Gibeonites, however, represent a minority group – with rights confirmed by covenant – treated, nevertheless, with clear hostility (see Joshua 9–10). Minority status applies to groups whose place under covenantal law remains ambiguous. While statistically some groups may actually represent a majority of individuals within a community, they become minorities because of their definition in the covenant. In this way certain racial groups sometimes defended, sometimes opposed, by Israelite writers represent minorities. Covenantal theology, at least as formulated in most sections of the Bible, grants theoretical respect and equality to minorities. In practical life, however, a tension between theory and reality results in hostility and often discrimination directed against such groups.

Perhaps no other minority group represents the possibilities inherent in the idea of covenant more than women. Jewish women have always been considered essential members of the covenanted people whose importance arises from within the community itself. The plight of women in Judaism may be generalized as an example of how minorities fare under the covenant, a test case for covenantal civil religion.

The modern period provides the most articulate expression of minority concerns by Jewish women. Jewish feminists raise important questions about Judaism and its traditional approach to women.[10] Men alone participate actively in the process of learning Torah. Many modern women claim that such favoritism degrades them and cheats the Jewish community of half its intellectual resources. Both men and women suffer by restricting Torah learning to one gender. Women offer insights and possibilities enhancing Jewish survival in the modern world.

Many Jews, male and female alike, have an ambivalent response to modern feminism. While they defend the rights of women as individuals, they are concerned about the public presence of women and their contention that their contributions to Torah be fully recognized. As long as Jewish women seek the right to a private piety, their wishes should be respected. When women desire to *davven* (recite the prayers) by themselves, form a woman's *minyan* (a prayer quorum), and voluntarily accept more personal religious obligations than those assigned to them, these Jews applaud their aims and desires. When women seek public recognition, however, the response changes. Women rabbis seem to be forcing themselves upon the Jewish public. Women who make loud public demands for changes in Jewish law that take cognizance of a woman's point of view (especially in such delicate questions as those of the *agunah* and abortion) become a nuisance. When women parade in public wearing *tallit* and *tefillin*, when they become conspicuous as rabbis, then many Jews are uncomfortable with feminism. Even when traditional Jews advance less revolutionary suggestions for increasing feminine participation in Jewish life, these approaches are rejected as subverting the *halakhic* process by which Jewish men have evolved Jewish law.[11]

A key to understanding the role of women within the covenant people, however, lies in understanding the various viewpoints expressed rather than polemically accepting the dogmatic statements made by any participants in the debate. From the earliest times women have acted as part of the Jewish community in a variety of ways. Some women have certainly opposed patriarchal authority, and in the face of their opposi-

tion some patriarchs have been discomfited. The story of Tamar
and Judah (Genesis 38) shows how a Canaanite woman taught
a Hebrew patriarch his obligations. Judah was forced to admit
that right was on the side of the woman.

This biblical tale demonstrates how one woman fulfilled the
feminine role of creative criticism. This critique is singularly
appropriate to the concept of covenant as civil religion. More
often than not it has been the male Jew who enjoys the rights
of citizenship, who exemplifies the civil ideal of the people,
while women have to pay the real consequences in daily disad-
vantages. The value of the modern movement for women's
liberation in Judaism includes an air of intellectual freshness,
as it brings new minds and bodies to the task of solving the
problems of Jewish life. Viewed from the perspective of Jewish
women, covenant as civil religion implies a different set of
expectations and obligations than when understood from a
traditional male vantage point.

Covenant as an inclusive civil religion must allow this non-
traditional viewpoint full expression. God speaks out through
the voices of these minorities; to remain indifferent to their
cries means to be indifferent to the divine. Abraham Heschel
interpreted the protest by black Americans in the 1960s as the
voice of God. Through their outrage Americans were
privileged to hear the divine demand that covenant community
respond to the needs of its members. With this in mind he
called the unrest "God's gift to America." God can be found
where communities recognize and heed a challenge to their
integrity, a protest from oppressed minorities.[12]

Covenant community requires an interactive system, not
merely channeled protest. Covenant duty includes the duty of
members of society to respect the integrity of the leadership.
Such a view has characterized many Jewish women who have
been deferential to established authority. Their role has been
to elucidate the meaning of covenant community through
stimulating Jews to self-examination and internal reflection.
The biblical example of the daughters of Zelophad (Num-

bers 27) demonstrates that Jewish institutions change according to the needs of the situation. The Israelites, about to enter the land of promise, employ a concept of an inalienable patrimony of land to ensure an economic equality among all members of the community, thus allowing greater access to interhuman encounters.

At first this economic policy applies only to male descendants in a family. The daughters of Zelophad approach Moses and complain against this sexist discrimination. As daughters they should inherit their father's property. The decision given in Numbers 27 universalizes the idea of a patrimony of land to enable daughters, no less than sons, to inherit from their fathers. Moses discovers, through attempting to redress the plight of women, that covenant expands the opportunities for human interaction only by overcoming prejudice and stereotypes. In this case, covenant obligation acts as a stimulus to greater inclusiveness for women, bringing the reality of communal life closer to the expectations promised.

Often a society, despite its commitment to an ideal and its openness to radical change as a means to attaining that goal, may also need to maintain certain well-defined roles and even discrimination between sexual groups. Women may represent an element of protest within Jewish life, but that protest may be redressed through social compromise rather than through activist revolution. Thus the daughters of Zelophad learn the importance of compromise (Numbers 36). This later passage reverses the implication of the earlier decision. The property goes to the women only if they marry within their own tribe. Here, radical change must give way to a more traditional viewpoint, not because of theoretical considerations, but because the real — less than ideal — conditions of society demand it. Access to interpersonal meeting needs to be integrated into the existing systems of human interaction. While one model of minority behavior suggests the necessity for protest, a second emphasizes the need for compromise when the very existence of social structures seems to depend upon it. Naturally, both

72 *Covenant and Community in Modern Judaism*

models may be abused — the first for self-serving favoritism and the second to justify repressive social institutions. Each exemplifies, however, a principle compatible with the other.

Many Jewish leaders claim that the *halahkic* distinction between men and women does not constitute discrimination in itself. The application of that distinction, however, has reflected the changing responses of Jews to their environment. The central justification for these changes comes less from the divine will they represent than from "the good sense of the Jewish people."[13] God's will, in this case, flows from consensus rather than protest. Jews seeking to find the divine presence in community should, on this reading, turn to the actual ways the Jewish community confronts its own internal problems. Civil religion institutes the will of the people as the expressive will of God, not as an authoritarian will, but as an evolving understanding of what is required for the survival of community as an open and responsive institution.

Sometimes, however, covenant requires women to assert their differences from men in a peculiarly gender-specific way. The story of Ruth represents still a third view of women given in the tradition. Ruth, a Moabite widow who accepts the God of Israel out of loyalty to her former husband's family, throws herself upon the mercy of Hebrew social convention. She seeks neither revolution nor justice but, rather, evokes merciful response from her kinsman Boaz. She receives the gleanings left for the poor, visits Boaz by night to plead for his compassion, and displays feminine virtues that call forth a caring love from protective men. Her reward comes through her progeny, since the great King David is one of her descendants. She epitomizes the traditional woman who sees her place within a family, who fastens her hopes upon a man, content to contribute to Jewish survival through her loyalty to the Jewish people and by performance of her biological functions.

Woman serves communal needs, on this account, by providing a link between the generations. She preserves the covenant just as she preserves the biological survival of the people through her gender-specific task. Two motivations merge to make women agree to this arrangement. The first is tribal loyalty. Women suffer when the nation as a whole suffers. Secondly, they achieve an important self-image from their role as tribal mothers. They enhance their status within the community as a whole and see their interconnection with the entire social body more clearly. Men recognize their (at least biological) dependence on women, and women articulate their indispensability for Jewish survival.

Ironically, however, Ruth fulfills this covenant purpose in a dramatically strange way. She is a non-Jew who enters into covenant community from the outside. She represents innovation that has been legitimated because it represents continuity. Ruth takes her future in her own hands and because she does so fulfills the patriarchal requirement of being a mother of the people.[14] God works through minorities to create a more traditional community, to ensure that innovation, when it occurs, will not conflict with but will reinforce communal ideals.

WOMEN AND THE MAKING OF COVENANT

God's pervading presence in minority protest, compromise, and traditionalism reflects the nature of covenant community. The stories told in Jewish tradition about covenant-making itself reflect this variety of responses to the place of minorities generally and women specifically in community. The various roles women play in the covenant people grow out of feminine participation in the task of covenant-making itself. The making of a covenant, according to the tradition, requires a unified, controversy-free Israel. The Torah was given at Sinai because the entire people camped as one. When covenant-making occurred, the tradition explains, both men and women were addressed equally. Perhaps more than equality is at stake, since some texts give primacy to women. Well-known midrashic passages (Exodus Rabba 28:2; Mekhilta Yitro: 1–2; and Talmud Shabbat 87a–b) note that when God commissioned

Moses to instruct Israel in the covenant, He commanded, "Speak to the House of Jacob, command the Sons of Israel" (Exodus 3:3). One of the various interpretations given this verse suggests that the former directive is for the women and the latter for the men.

This midrash proved problematic for Jewish thinkers. Why should women be addressed first? Does God regard them more or less highly than men are regarded? A number of explanations are then devised to explain women's precedence: they receive the divine message first because they were loyal during the temptation of the golden calf, because they are more active in pursuing the commandments, because they instruct their children in the ways of Torah. Taken this way, the midrashic explanation of the verse considers women as activist partners in the making of covenant, even more active than the men. The activist woman asserts women's active contribution to covenantal living.

This activist tradition, however, has been mitigated in several important rabbinic passages. No sooner had the midrash mentioned above been accepted than it was surrounded by explanatory addenda that changed its meaning. Women were not to be activists but to articulate the general principles of Jewish life, principles that men translate into detailed practice. A later tradition, originally independent of the midrash giving precedence to women (see the way the interpretation is given in Mekhilta), claims that the first part of Exodus 3:3 refers to "the principles" of Torah while the latter refers to the "details." As *Exodus Rabba* develops the interpretation of the verse, however, the two traditions are merged. The women are instructed first, in the general principles of the Torah most suitable for feminine understanding; the men are then provided with the detailed instruction needed for their masculine tasks.

According to this midrash, the Jewish people make up a community illustrating certain general principles of human behavior. The principle of the separation of the sexes and their equal, but different, tasks, is included among those principles illustrated. Thus, women participate in covenant-making through their grasp of the broad basic commitments required by Torah. These principles include a division of labor sometimes associated with specific genders. The community fosters human interaction by providing its members with clear guidelines for behavior. Such role models prevent chaos and support individuals in their often challenging efforts to encounter one another as full human beings. The extraordinary aspect of woman's task is the feminine representation of various ideals in their pristine, clearly articulated form. This task requires that women, in their very essence, stand for a reality different from that of men and therefore includes some activities common with men, excludes certain actions appropriate only for men, and provides special commandments for women alone. While the making of covenant requires a unity between principles and details, the fulfilling of covenant requires that different groups accept different tasks. While non-activist, this view—in which women by their essential nature teach men values that are otherwise inaccessible to them—does emphasize that community must enable human meetings. By each member of society embodying a particular value, the community also values the interaction of individuals so that the full system of values becomes clear. Men teach women what they have discovered through social experience; women instruct men in their peculiar discoveries. This teaching function complements the activist tradition.

The rabbinic tradition includes a third view of women's participation in the covenant-making event that formed Jewish community. Women fulfill a biological task—that of ensuring the survival of the Jewish people. A renowned tale suggests that God offered the Jews the Torah only on the condition that they provide some collateral on that loan. The men offered various possible securities—gold, silver, the sun and moon—none of which were acceptable. Then the women offered their children as collateral and were immediately accepted. Women enable the covenant to continue by their function as childbearers who offer their offspring as security for the promise God makes to Israel. The contrast offered here is startling. Men are locked into materialistic concerns; they assume that community has as its purpose the accumulation of goods. Women, however, see more clearly. They recognize that community exists to foster human relationships and that as such its members are its most prized possession. This insight into the very nature of covenant community suggests the priority of women in the midrashic consciousness even if their role seems to be restricted to that of childbearer and preserver of the physical community.

From this perspective, women, more than men, stand for the rationale and purpose of entering into covenant with God. The activist tradition may understand women's role in Judaism more creatively, and the teaching tradition may see women as more persuasive, but neither gives women more intrinsic importance for communal life than does this emphasis on Jewish survival.

WOMEN AND JEWISH COVENANT COMMUNITY TODAY

The tradition's own multi-valent approach to the place of women within the people of the covenant is reflected in a variety of theologies. That approach evolves out of a series of concerns, all them included in the Kotzker's desire for "natural community." As Buber suggests, community and its political forms represent a means, not an end, a tool for creating a responsive environment. In the case of each model — whether that of Tamar, the daughters of Zelophad, of Ruth — or of the place of women in making the covenant, the test depends less on preconceived notions of political ideals than on interhuman concerns. Because life and Judaism engage in an ongoing dialogue, no one expression of Judaism can be final.

George E. Johnson, criticizing Jewish women for having rejected traditional role models and institutions without creating any new ones, claims that the radicality of feminism under-mines the *halakhic* seriousness of the movement among Jewish women.[15] This view misunderstands the pluralistic nature of covenant and the variety of ways in which minority groups contribute to communal life. The place of Jewish women within the covenant community represents the variety of ways in which minorities can be integrated into the whole of the Jewish people. The covenant does make the survival of Jews and Judaism a primary consideration. For that survival minorities must sacrifice self-interest for the good of the whole no less than the majority population must cultivate the welfare of minority members. That sacrifice of self-interest, however, should not be regarded as entirely negative. Self-worth and personal esteem grow out of such actions performed for the good of all. The minority's acceptance of a specified role within the whole should not be construed as discrimination. Many minority groups choose to accept a distinctive task, a peculiar identity, that gives them a status of their own.

The covenant establishes a civil religion not only to unify the community but also to provide a variety of ways in which minorities such as women may have access to interhuman relationships. Marginal communities in general have the unique advantage of being able to look at the social whole from a double perspective — they recognize both the ideals animating the group and the failure to reach those ideals in practice. Minority groups within Judaism often serve just this function of being guardians of ideals that are often honored more in the breach than in the practice, just as women often articulate ideals that men have ignored.

No community can endure if it does not incorporate new patterns of response to a changing world. Traditional Judaism, because of its defensive stand and because of the primacy of survival in a hostile environment, often muted this aspect of Jewish life. Nonetheless, as a covenant community committed to expanding possibilities for human encounters, Jewish tradi-tion retained elements of flexibility. The various trends found in that tradition concerning the place of women in the making of covenant show the possibility of integrating minority expressions into the creative process. The task set by covenant — that of opening ever wider spheres for interhuman meeting — entails a respect for diversity, variation, and creativity, and the opportunities for minorities are equally varied. Thus covenant as civil religion represents an inclusive model.

NOTES

1.   Martin Buber, *Between Man and Man*, with an afterword by the author and an introduction by Maurice Friedman, trans. Ronald Gregor Smith and Maurice Friedman (New York: Macmillan, 1965), p. 31.

2.   Buber, *Tales of the Hasidim: Later Masters*, trans. Olga Marx (New York: Schocken, 1961), pp. 39 and 289.

3.   Ibid., p. 44; see the entire discussion of the Kotzker on pp. 39–44.

4.   Buber, *Hasidism and Modern Man*, ed. and trans. Maurice Friedman (New York: Horizon Press, 1958), p. 167.

5.   See Robert N. Bellah, *Beyond Belief: Essays on Religion in a Post-Traditional World* (New York: Harper and Row, 1970), pp. 168–89; see also Bellah's, *The Broken Covenant: American Civil Religion in Time of Trial* (New York: Seabury Press, 1975), pp. 151–52.

6.   Buber, *Hasidism and Modern Man*, p. 166.

7.   Buber, *Between Man and Man*, pp. 7, 80.

8.   See Buber, *Moses: The Revelation and the Covenant* (New York: Harper and Row, 1958), pp. 187–89.

9.   See Buber, *On Zion: The History of An Idea*, with a new foreword by Nahum N. Glatzer, trans. Stanley Grafman, (London: Horowitz, 1973); Buber, *Israel and the World: Essays in a Time of Crisis*, 2d ed. (New York: Schocken, 1963); and Buber, *A Land of Two Peoples: Martin Buber on Jews and Arabs* (New York: Oxford University Press, 1983).

10.   See Rachel Adler, "The Jew Who Wasn't There: Halacha and the Jewish Woman," in *Contemporary Jewish Ethics*, ed. Menahem Marc Kellner (New York: Sanhedrin Press, 1978), pp. 347–99; Ruth F. Brin, "Can a Woman Be a Jew?" in *A Coat of Many Colors: Jewish Subcommunities in the United States*, ed. Abraham D. Lavender (Westport, Conn.: Greenwood Press, 1977), pp. 243–51; Paula Hyman, "The Other Half: Women in the Jewish Tradition," *Conservative Judaism* 26 (1972), pp. 14–21; and Cynthia Ozick, "Women: Notes Toward Finding the Right Questions," *Forum* 35 (1979), pp. 37–60. The most sustained and detailed study on the place of women and suggestions for future development can be found in Blu Greenberg, *On*

Women and Judaism: A View from Tradition (Philadelphia: Jewish Publication Society of America, 1981).

11. See such works as Reuben P. Bulka, "Women's Role: Some Ultimate Concerns," *Tradition* 17 (1979), pp. 27–40; Raziel Schnall Friedfertig and Freyda Schapiro, eds., *The Modern Jewish Woman: A Unique Perspective* (Boston: Lubavitch Education Foundation, 1981); George E. Johnson, "Halakha and Women's Liberation," *Midstream* 20 (1974), pp. 58–61; Ralph Pelcovitz, "Women's Lib in Torah Perspective," in *Danger and Opportunity* (New York: Shengold Publishers, 1976), pp. 111–22; and responses to Blu Greenberg's previously cited book by Naomi Englard-Schaffer, *Tradition* 21 (1983), pp. 132–45 and by Emanuel Feldman, *Tradition* 22 (1984), pp. 98–106.

12. See Abraham Joshua Heschel, *The Insecurity of Freedom: Essays on Human Existence* (New York: Schocken, 1972), pp. 85–111.

13. See the discussion in Zvi Kurzweil, "The Equality of Women," in *The Modern Impulse of Traditional Judaism* (Hoboken, N.J.: Ktav, 1985), pp. 117–23.

14. See the discussion by Phyllis Trible in *God and the Rhetoric of Sexuality* (Philadelphia: Fortress, 1978).

15. Johnson, "Halakha and Women's Liberation."

5

Inclusive Covenant

TOWARDS AN INCLUSIVE COVENANT

Covenantal theology runs a risk of parochialism, of focusing on individuals searching for identity and on the dynamics of civil organization. From earliest times Jews have been accused of clannishness, parochialism, and exclusivism. The idea of covenant, however, contains enough ambivalence to justify a variety of interpretations.[1] The assertion that a special agreement, a contract, or treaty joins the divine and human in a unique relationship may lead to exclusivism, to an intensely self-centered concern. The particularistic or parochial focus of covenant seems appropriate as Jews seek to discover the meaning of their lives, to decode personal significance, and to uncover their unique contribution to humanity. The covenantal search for identity creates a necessary and defensible parochialism.

Covenant as the constitution of a dynamic society, however, emphasizes pluralism and legitimates diverse institutions striving to reach similar goals. While one aspect of covenant stresses parochialism, another focuses on how a covenantal paradigm justifies evolution, change, and a plurality of civil models. Thus the biblical corpus contains a variety of covenants, suggesting that any single covenant (that with Noah or Abraham or Moses or David or Ezra) requires a complementary covenant either before or after it. No one covenant community exhausts the meaning of God's relationship to humanity. The declaration of Amos, "Are not you Israelites like the Ethiopians to me? says the LORD" (Amos 9:7), reflects such a consideration. Such a view emphasizes pluralism. A plurality of covenants suggests that diverse groups have equal claim to relationship with the divine through such an agreement.

Beyond the parochialism of covenant as an affirmation of distinctiveness and the pluralism of covenant as justification for a variety of covenantal communities, covenant sometimes appears as a promise for the future. The Jewish Bible in its structure, for example, symbolizes this approach. The Torah concludes with Moses on the edge of the promised land. The Israelites have not yet crossed into the land of the covenant; the ideal remains in the future, not yet finished. The Prophets end with the eschatological promise of the Book of Malachi — God will send Elijah the prophet to reconcile all humanity. The Writings, as preserved in modern Jewish Bibles, reverse historical chronology. The four books, 1 and 2 Chronicles and Ezra and Nehemiah, retell the biblical story from the creation of the world through the Judean return to the land of promise from exile in Babylonia. Chronologically the books of Ezra and Nehemiah conclude the Chronicler's history. The Jewish Bible, however, rearranges the order of the books and ends with 2 Chronicles, a book concluding with a forward-looking promise that Jews would be allowed to return to their homeland. The shape of the Hebrew canon, then, suggests a futuristic implication in covenantal expectations.

Covenant in this "futuristic" sense points to an ideal reality, an extended human community not yet existing but maintained as an ideal. This ideal, stated unambiguously in the prophetic books, culminates in Malachi. The essential covenantal obligation, according to this perspective, demands those who accept it to work towards a perfected human world. The obligations entailed extend beyond specific directives. The general imperative requires dedication to realizing an improved human order. The expectation of a unified world, of an inclusive community of humanity, promised by covenant represents a possibility not yet achieved.

At the heart of this expectation lies a statement about the divine in relationship to the world. This view conditions a reading of Malachi 2:10–11, "Have we all not one father? Has not one God created us? Why do we violate the covenant of our forefathers by being faithless to one another?"[2] The rabbis wonder why the recitation of the *Shema*, the declaration of God's unity in Deuteronomy 6:4, should be followed liturgically by the expression "Praised be the glory of His Kingdom forever and ever." One interpretation refers to the verse in Malachi. When human beings recognize their kinship and act covenantally with one another, then God's kingdom will be established. God's unity becomes the presupposition upon which Jews build the hope for a united human community. Covenantal obligation, then, becomes the demand to expand the consciousness of individuals and communities to see the inherent relatedness of all human beings. The covenantal expectation promises a new human order based upon that awareness. God's presence may be sensed in the preconditions that make the reality of human interrelatedness obvious.

Covenant as a futuristic program implies three related imperatives. The first imperative focuses on a changed attitude towards the world. Rather than taking a self-centered or even an ethnocentric view of reality, covenant thinking demands a more universal point of view. Compassion for all creation, concern for the world in its own right, must replace selfishness.

Sometimes only crisis can create this compassion. Only suffering itself sensitizes individuals and groups to the pain of humanity. Abraham Heschel understood this when he declared—as indicated in the previous chapter—that the crisis among black Americans was a blessing for the United States. That crisis created an awareness of human interdependence, of shared pain, of a common burden. God blessed America, one might say, by allowing it to experience such a healing sorrow.

Heschel's perspective reflects his contention that individuals and societies must recognize their potential for action. He claimed that in any situation "some are guilty, but all are responsible."3 Just as covenantal meaning assumes personal free will, so futuristic covenant assumes that human beings can create their own futures. The covenantal expectation in this case points to social activism. Compassion alone does not transform the world. That compassion needs to be channeled and directed into specific deeds. Those deeds require active human beings, not merely passive acceptance of a status quo.

The final imperative of a futuristic covenant demands an optimistic and inclusive attitude towards human nature. On the one hand, humanity requires the framework of an extended community for its self-realization. On the other hand, every human being possesses the potential for creating and maintaining just such an extended communal consciousness. Thus covenant as futuristic affirms an optimistic view of reality. Human beings can develop more and more inclusive ways of thinking and acting. While much divides one community from another, and much separates individuals even within a society, a futuristic covenant contends that there is a basic commonality that unites humanity.

An example of such optimistic covenantal thinking occurs in a saying attributed to Rabbi Akiva Ben Joseph, a second-century Jewish leader (Avot 3:13–16). Akiva called humanity blessed for being created in the image of God and even more blessed for being made aware of that fact; he called Israel specially blessed for being the sons of God and more specially blessed in being made aware of that status. Jacob Neusner is right to note that the emphasis in this saying is neither on creation in the image of God nor on specific Jewish chosenness, but rather on the importance of human awareness.4

The consequence of such awareness lies in the social obligations that follow from it. Jews, having been made aware of their special task, have social obligations towards one another, while, as the statement makes clear, Jews have a special obligation to other Jews born of the covenant at Sinai. The first part of Akiva's statement, however, means that Jews share a common goal with all humanity and a common task — that of living up to the image of God, which they represent.

Covenantal task implies recognizing this universal obligation, of bringing to consciousness the full awareness of human interrelatedness. For Jews, exile among the nations has stimulated this awareness and consciousness. As strangers in a strange land, as resident aliens in foreign countries, Jews have learned to reaffirm humanity's interconnectedness. A longstanding tradition declares that Jews are responsible for the welfare of the society within which they reside just as that society is itself responsible for the welfare of its Jewish residents. Jeremiah's instruction to the exiles of his time (Jeremiah 29:7) urged them to "pray for the welfare of the country" to which they had been dispersed. Jews have taken that injunction seriously. Cooperation between Jew and non-Jew grows out of a basic realization that humanity represents a single community, that the fate of one individual or group affects all others. A future orientation refuses to accept the hostilities dividing communities as unchangeable. Jews who affirm a covenantal image of the future transcend exclusivism and participate energetically in intergroup dialogue. Recognizing that present conditions require transformation according to covenantal directives, Jews join others willingly struggling to meet the challenges of a less than perfect world. Since all human beings participate in "the image of God," each must work to make that hidden image manifest. Each does so, however, in dialogue and companionship with others.

COMPASSION AND UNIVERSALISM IN JEWISH COVENANT

The primary covenantal obligation from this futuristic perspective entails a sense of unity, an inclusiveness that expands outward from the covenantal affirmations of self and society. This balance of universalism and particularism characterizes the orientation of Jewish theology generally. Shmuel Hugo Bergman makes it clear that the two poles of Jewish thinking — chosenness and messianism — combine in covenant obligation. The community must survive because the universal mission of Judaism depends upon social action rather than the deeds of solitary individuals.[5] Throughout Jewish tradition, then, the tension between the particular and the universal has been reduced by seeing one as the function of the other. Through their particularity, the Jewish people become a catalyst for a mission that affects all humanity. Jewish particularism does not breed exclusivism but points to a more inclusive Jewish task, the task of awakening humanity to its common ancestry in the divine and its kinship relationship, which demands mutual responsibility.

This view of Judaism often conditions how theologians interpret the tradition. When Abraham Joshua Heschel turns to the stories of the Kotzker Rebbe, for example, he understands those stories in the context of the universal Jewish mission. Since the Kotzker's purpose appears to be that of a prophet recalling people to true worship, Heschel retells the tale of the quest for disciples from this perspective. He recasts that story on the model of Elijah's confrontation with the priests of Baal on Mount Carmel (1 Kings 18). As Heschel explains it, the Kotzker was besieged by multitudes of admirers. He rejected this popularity and declared that all he required were a few hundred men to stand with him and shout from the rooftops, "The Lord He is God." This outburst of genuine piety on the part of a few disciples would be able to transform the world.[6] The Kotzker sought disciples who would imitate the daring of Elijah, a band of prophetic followers. Like Elijah they would confront all who worship idols. Like him they would succeed in having all the world admit that "the Lord is God." Such a universal declaration implies responsibility to humanity as a whole, not just to the Jewish people. Heschel contends that the Kotzker's agony extended to include all injustice, that he would agonize over Hiroshima and Nagasaki no less than over the holocaust.[7] His compassion did not end with concern for Jews but embraced all suffering humanity.

Heschel attributes the Kotzker's desire for disciples to his compassion. His resolution to "work on the hardest stone" sent him "looking for a few surging people." Certainly the Kotzker's efforts did not result in a mass movement; he attracted only a few followers. Only "some" could learn "to overcome the deception found above ground."[8] Such a minimal following does not imply failure. While Wiesel considers the Kotzker an example of the absurdity of human existence, and Buber concludes that the Kotzker failed, pointing the way to experiments that would not fail, Heschel argues that the Kotzker succeeded. His protest did not go unheard. In his own time a few answered his call. In modern times both Jews and non-Jews may respond to his continuing summons. His contemporary significance remains a testimony to his success. "The Kotzker continues," Heschel maintains, "to stand before us as a soul aflame with passion for God. . . . His words throw flames whenever they come into our orbit."[9] The Kotzker's teaching of compassion remains a powerful and successful witness for modern humanity.

As Heschel tells the story of the Kotzker, success cannot be measured by immediate effects. Religious teachings, from the Bible onwards, continue to be relevant long after their creation. Menahem Mendel stands within a prophetic heritage linking the Bible to the present day. Modern Jews may still respond to the Kotzker's dream; they may answer his call for "surging individuals." Today's world, like the Kotzker's, requires a few hundred men to climb to the rooftops and shout out truth, to remind people of the horrors they perpetrate by indifference and callousness. Whereas it might be thought that four hundred disciples represent the minimum necessary for transforming the world, it may be a metaphor pointing to the faithful few. If only a few hundred people understand the vulnerability of human existence and compassionately reach out to others, the Kotzker has accomplished his purpose. The model of the Kotzker's extreme compassion and intense concerns remains an effective religious statement for human beings today.

Heschel explains the Kotzker's desire to "lift up the heavens" as an attempt to motivate religious intensity without parochialism, to assert a human task without also descending into egotistic solipsism. By focusing on an active task oriented beyond the self, the Kotzker prevented spirituality itself from becoming self-indulgent. A religious life centered on personal salvation makes the self into an idol.[10] The Kotzker refused to limit his hope for salvation to that of the isolated Jewish individual. He even dared to hope for a redemption that transcended the Jewish people alone. In this way, the Kotzker introduced a model of universalism, representing the broad compassion for all humanity demanded by convenantal duty. He moved beyond the particularity of Judaism to encompass the whole world, suggesting a model for contemporary Jews. This model of universalism represents one element in the obligations of covenant—the element of a broadly human compassion.

Heschel understands this aspect of the Kotzker well. Menahem Mendel's radical stance converted the particular religious duties of the Jew into expressions of a generally human concern—sympathy with all who suffer in the universe. Jews, he contends, should share pain wherever it occurs and to whomever it strikes. The Kotzker argued that not only the individual involved suffers pain; whenever a creature suffers, the creator also feels pain. Jews should imitate this divine passion. They should feel the same sorrow and distress that afflicts each suffering being. In this way, the Kotzker claims, Jews emulate divine compassion on the world and fulfill a major covenantal obligation by sympathizing with God's suffering. Heschel uses this idea to explain the Kotzker's analogy of the world to a house on fire. If it is burning up and no one cares for it, then the owner of the house must also be indifferent to its fate. Menahem Mendel recognized that God cared deeply that His house was in flames. True worship, in his mind, meant sharing that profound suffering, having compassion for a creator tormented by His creatures' torment. Such an imperative towards compassion represents an important message for modern humanity.

Covenant becomes an ecumenical structure when Jews recognize their fellowship in suffering with others. The Nazi holocaust, ironically, seems to have stimulated such sympathetic understanding. Covenant as a mode of empathy with others seems particularly appropriate in the modern world, a world whose inhabitants join a fellowship of suffering. Jewish thinkers recognize the opportunities for dialogue offered in this contemporary setting. Jews and Christians alike stand isolate in a culture that seems to deny human value, that avoids confronting human suffering. When Jews take their experience of the holocaust as a point of departure for any human dialogue, they create the possibility for transcending selfishness.

Human community today extends beyond the narrow confines of parochialism. New opportunities and new challenges have arisen. Religion has become a voluntary, chosen way of response rather than an inherited and inevitable aspect of life. Religious leaders are more vulnerable than ever before, and thus religion provides a useful mirror for human vulnerability. Irving Greenberg notes that contemporary suffering, the struggle to give meaning to the absurd tragedies of our times, has transformed religious traditions. Religious leaders have learned to identify themselves with the oppressed and become open to the alienated — the women, the "deviant," the excluded of society.[11] Religious expectations and obligations may suggest a new framework for human cooperation, for interhuman communication, a framework based upon compassion. That new framework suggests an often neglected reality of life: all human suffering is interconnected. When any part of the cosmos is in pain, all parts feel the torment.

Jewish teachings symbolize this idea by alluding to divine passion, to God's suffering with the world. This compassionate divine suffering finds striking expression in the idea of the *Shekinah*.[12] Where Jews gather in the name of God, there the *Shekinah*, the indwelling presence, joins them. Thus when Jews are suffering in exile, the *Shekinah* goes with them to share the pain and suffering of the people. Whenever a Jew is hurt, then the *Shekinah* cries out "My head is being hurt! My hand is in pain!" To round off the cycle of mutuality Jews are told not to complain of personal pain. If they have a headache they are to cry, "The head of the *Shekinah* is in pain." If they suffer they are to lament, "O, for the suffering of the *Shekinah*." Compassion for suffering grows into identification with the deity.

COVENANTAL ACTIVISM: MOVING BEYOND COMPASSION

Compassion alone may be passive and inactive. Heschel suggests that the Kotzker rejected a compassion that accepted the status quo. He comments that the Kotzker will not accept "satisfaction with the status quo" or being "indifferent to atrocity." Such reconciliation to life, according to Heschel, "repudiates the validity of waiting for the Messiah."[13]

This view might be called "messianic ethics." The messianic vision of a better world vitalizes human activity, stimulates an ethical dynamism. Messianism, the future orientation towards a fulfilled ideal for humanity, often appears to be a passive response to human suffering. Jews, some authors argue, turn to the hope of a messianic redeemer because they have become disenchanted with the possibilities of normal life. Messianism may be an escape into fantasy. Disappointments plague the Jewish people as they seek to fulfill their mission. Messianism evolved in response to those disappointments. When realistic hopes fail, people turn to fantastic expectations. Gershom Scholem, who combines his expertise in Jewish mysticism with a commitment to Zionism, advocates this position. He suggests that Jewish messianic hopes were a utopianism borne out of failure. "The magnitude of the messianic idea," he argues, "corresponds to the endless powerlessness in Jewish history during all the centuries of the exile."[14] If this view is right, if universalism and compassion merely reflect powerlessness, they must be rejected in favor of a more realistic activism. Jewish nationalists make a persuasive argument for their case. They contend that neither the creation of a peculiarly Jewish world view nor an experiment with Jewish communal organizations can occur without Jewish autonomy. Such nationalists refuse the comfort offered by traditional messianism. The future orientation and universalism of that position seem passive and the products of generations when Jews lacked political power. Messianism, according to this view, grew as an aberration born of political weakness, a projecting of autonomy to the end of time because Jews lack the strength of character to succeed in obtaining it in the real world of everyday life.

Such a view, however, mistakes the delayed vision of Jewish success for temporizing and considers modern movements such as Zionism legitimate replacements for traditional Jewish activism. The Zionist alternative recognizes the covenantal obligation for action rather than passivity. By focusing only on the parochial tasks associated with covenant as a personal world view or covenant as a paradigm for social organization, they overlook the futuristic aspects of Judaism. Covenant entails belief in an ideal not yet realized, an ideal that transcends any concrete actuality—whether that actuality be the individual or the community. Taking the futuristic element in covenantal religion seriously means respecting the messianic impulse. The messianic ideal voices the contention that no covenantal institution should look only at specifically Jewish concerns, that the welfare of the entire human world, not just of Jewish life, remains a crucial test of covenantal loyalty. Only if the obligations of covenant create universal expectations will the sphere of activity they initiate be a realm in which the universal God who suffers with all humanity participates. Jews envision the messianic ideal stimulating activism.

Among the leading exponents of such messianic thinking in

rabbinic times was Rabbi Joshua ben Levi. The Talmudic tales about Rabbi Joshua ben Levi intimate that his orientation developed from a focus on a mystical world view to include concern for the people of Israel, for the social structure of his community. A final hint, however, suggests that he eventually transcended even this parochialism to achieve a universalism expressed in messianic activism. Rabbinic sources describe Rabbi Joshua ben Levi as a mystic who had frequent visions in which Elijah the prophet came to tutor him. He was an ascetic who mastered the secret lore of kabbalistic magic and who sought self-perfection.

On one of his excursions into the heavenly realm, he asked whether he would be admitted into the world to come on his death. Elijah refused to answer but said instead, "Go to the Messiah, and he will tell you." When Rabbi Joshua inquired after the Messiah, he found that the Messiah was a beggar sitting at the gates of Rome, suffering countless ills and diseases. Journeying to Rome, Rabbi Joshua discovered the pitiful condition of the Jewish people and learned that suffering and sorrow were the condition of his nation. And so when he reached the Messiah he forgot entirely about the purpose of his mission. He greeted the Messiah, "Peace be upon you, my Rabbi." The Messiah replied, "Peace be upon you, O, son of Levi." Rabbi Joshua then asked, "When will you come to save the Jewish people?" The Messiah answered, "Today!" Rabbi Joshua waited, but the Messiah did not come to redeem Israel. He complained to Elijah, who explained that the Messiah meant to quote the verse in Psalm 95: "Today, if you would heed my voice." At that point Elijah asked Rabbi Joshua how the Messiah had addressed him. Hearing that the Messiah had greeted him as "Son of Levi," Elijah declared, "Both you and your father are assured of a place in the world to come."[15] Now that Joshua has achieved a knowledge of messianic activism, he has redeemed both himself and his entire community.

Rabbi Joshua's sensitivity to the messianic vision evolves by stages in this story. At first he seems wrapped up in his own private world. He is concerned with achieving eternal life, with winning acceptance into the "true world." His quest for the Messiah, however, leads him into a different world, into a confrontation with the facticity of pain, suffering, and despair. This encounter leads him to recognize that his own needs must be put aside for those of the Jewish people as a whole. His question of the Messiah reflects his new perspective. When will communal life change, he asks; when will a new social order arise. His disappointed political hopes, however, lead Rabbi Joshua to discover that the transformation of the world depends upon him. His recognition of that point justifies both his private concerns and his communal ones. Both he and his father are legitimated. By taking on the activism of listening to God's commandments, he advances to a more universalistic stage and as such gains both his original desire and his second goal as well. He learns that he can create a world, he can establish a personal reality through what he achieves. He also realizes that by his activism he can legitimate and justify the existence of the Jewish people and their social experimentation. A sense of both personal value and social activism are essential ingredients in the ultimate redemption of the world, but only when animated by a universal concern, by an activism that takes the needs of all humanity seriously. The messianic approach to covenant obligation unites personal self-affirmation and communal realism into an optimistic struggle to create the ideal vision of a unified human world.

COVENANTAL LAW AND INCLUSIVE COMMUNITY

An inclusive covenant, therefore, builds upon the presuppositions of covenant understood as a personal vision of reality and as a plurality of social institutions. Compassion, vitalized by activism, channels both personal vision and the specific political paradigms evolved in a certain time and place. Joshua ben Levi discovered that his activism in regard to both personal and social desires could lead to universalism through attention to divine commandments, to the imperatives of Jewish tradition. What specific deeds lead to this improved, redeemed humanity? What type of human living responds most productively to the suffering and pain of existence and thereby legitimates a private world view and public institutions?

In the midst of his discussion of the Kotzker, Abraham Heschel distinguishes three ways in which Jews have focused on the problem of human existence: what a person should or should not do, what a person should or should not think, and "what one thinks while acting."[16] The Kotzker emphasized that deeds alone and piety by itself were incomplete. They become true religion only when animated by a universalistic impulse. While the specific forms of Jewish deeds may be conditioned by culture and history, the ideals to which they point are universal. Once, it is told, a disciple approached Rabbi Menahem Mendel lamenting that he did not possess a prayer shawl, the fringed garment required by tradition. The rebbe became furious. Why did the disciple need the fringed garment at all? The shawl only acted as a symbol reminding Jews to bind together the fragmented parts of the universe. "Wrap yourself in the four corners of the earth," the Kotzker stormed. "Then you will not need to worry about wrapping yourself in a fringed garment."[17] The symbol of world unity may be replaced by a compassionate recognition of the reality symbolized. This aspect of the Kotzker's approach demonstrates an emphatic activism combined with a sensitivity to all of humanity. Covenant obligation entails compassion and deeds conjoined by dedication to a universal task. The parochial forms of Jewish worship and ritual symbolize generally human values that must become realized in an ecumenical setting. The meaning of traditional performances transcends the inherited forms and points to concerns that should animate not only Jewish life but all human living.

The covenant as a futuristic ideal points to a time when not only Jews but all humanity will fulfill the intentions that vitalize Jewish law. When the laws of the Torah are understood as the means by which certain humanistic intentions may be realized, they lose their particularistic character. These laws, Jewish thinkers often proclaim, do not merely create a better world for all humanity. They point the way to a fulfilled and fulfilling life for every individual. This idea finds expression in Leviticus 18:5: "These are the laws that a person must do and live." This text has been taken to mean that human needs, requirements for personal or communal survival, take priority over ritual considerations. Covenant obligation enhances life by creating that social situation most conducive to human fulfillment. The laws of communal obligation found in the Torah have one object — the making of true human existence a reality.

This statement from the Pentateuch needs to be looked at carefully. While focused on a specific covenantal contract — that given to the Jewish people — the implications reach beyond it. At one level, the verse suggests the contractual aspect of covenant: those who fulfill the obligations set for them will gain their expectations of a prosperous life. Another level of meaning, however, suggests that the criterion for determining the meaning of covenant law lies in its effectiveness, in its universal intentions. The Talmudic sage, Rabbi Meir, noted that the Hebrew words used indicate that every human being is intended: not just a priest, not just a levite, not just an Israelite, but any person who fulfills the divine task receives the divine reward — life itself.[18] The obligations of covenant apply not just to Jews but to all human beings; the expectation of covenantal reward transcends any particular human community to include the human family as a whole.

The covenantal image, interpreted in this way, extends to every human individual and every human group. Such an image has immediate relevance for both Jews and non-Jews. It suggests that the central concern of any human community should be not its own self-interest but that of all humanity. The laws are not given for the sake of any particular cultural group but as models for every human collectivity. Since the laws point to generally human concerns, society should take the good of humanity as its most important objective.

From this perspective, community may begin in parochialism, but through the monotheistic image it extends outward to the entire human race. Just as a specific cultural community may be related to one another through mutual responsibilities, so too each individual reaches out to every other individual person. Corporate responsibility extends beyond one community to embrace all communities.

This expectation that human beings may eventually recognize their unity in diversity, their common goals despite their separate paths to them, evolves from a growing religious consciousness. A variety of psychologists have attempted to devise a hierarchy of "stages of faith."[19] Such an "evolutionary" approach, based on limited data and often very broad generalizations, needs to be used with great caution. Most of these works, however, despite a great variety in description of the exact stages of religious development, agree that expanding human consciousness and the opportunity for interhuman encounter provides an important evaluative key. James Fowler, for example, claims that the norm used for evaluating the development of faith should be that "each new stage expands the capacities of the person or community of faith."[20] Such a view suggests that a mature or evolving community should be one that increases personal and social opportunities. While resisting the impulse to develop a system for categorizing stages or types of religion, a student of covenantal community may utilize the criterion of growing possibilities. Covenant acts to create community best, it may be argued, when it opens new avenues of living, providing new options for human interaction.

The optimism of this paradigm needs to be tempered with caution. Covenantal obligations presuppose the need for human change and self-improvement. The messianic, futuristic aspects of inclusive covenant recognize that even the best, the most "mature," of religious options must cope with suffering and pain. Perhaps the most important and ecumenical aspects of futuristic covenant lie in this realism that does not assure success. Covenant demands that Jews recognize the difficulties involved in responding to human sorrow compassionately. The primary obligation is this recognition of pain combined with active measures to alleviate it. The future orientation of covenant, however, acknowledges that the external forms of Jewish symbolism may need to be expanded. If the four corners of the earth substitute for the fringes of the prayer shawl, so universalism may replace parochialism.

Incorporating elements from non-Jewish symbolism need not mean accepting them as normative or including them as aspects of Judaism itself. These symbols may be reminders of the world of others with whom Jews share the cosmos. Maurice Friedman, for example, cites the Kotzker Rebbe in just such a context. He notes that Rabbi Mendel emphasized the value of controversies: controversies for the sake of heaven endure. When Jews recognize that others also strive for the same goals, they can accept difference as part of a common human effort. Friedman affirms that it is possible "to confirm the other in his truth even while opposing him," and argues that "we do not have to liberate the world from those who have different witnesses from us."[21] A messianic covenantal awareness will recognize the need to keep the symbols of these "different witnesses" alive. True human community develops only in an atmosphere of meeting and encounter. Since the covenant points to a future of unity, Jews must learn even now to accept others in their differences.

Achieving this goal may require the creation of a "civil religion" that acknowledges the reality of diverse paths to common goals through its inclusive symbolism; a futuristic covenant hastens the realization of its vision. Understood as a complement, not a replacement, of the particular expressions of Jewish religion, as an addition to rather than a displacement of personal identity and political self-awareness, Rubenstein's advocacy of a universal symbolism does not conflict with Jewish teachings. Covenant obligation requires an awareness of what gives others pain. Only when a messianic ideal is already attained would any community be justified in restricting covenantal membership to those who accept a specific set of symbols and practices. The realism of covenantal hope suggests that ecumenical sharing in this pain-filled world offers a valid path to the realization of futuristic covenantal expectations.

When diverse communities listen openly and honestly to one another they create the basis for a futuristic hope, for a common sense of community. Naturally this community will have its own symbols, perhaps drawn from common sources. These symbols may provide a vocabulary for interfaith communication. Dialogue with other communities fulfills the obligation of futuristic covenant understood as a commitment to universalism, an acceptance of the duties flowing from compassion combined with activism. As modern Jews engage in interfaith dialogue they exemplify this covenantal paradigm by demonstrating an attitude of shared concern, of vital activism, and of ecumenical awareness that the intentions of Jewish law may be common even when the details of that law are not. An anonymous medieval Jewish moralist once asked how it is possible for a person to be trained to love others. The reply was to seek to become as useful as possible to all people.[22] Compassion between communities stimulates the desire to be helpful to others, and provides training in the ability to love. Covenant, understood as a paradigm of interaction between communities, obligates one group to be concerned with the welfare of another. These obligations aim toward a universal social order in which distinctive cultures converse openly, creating a dialogue in which covenantal faith perceives the presence of God.

NOTES

1.   The ideas that follow have been stimulated by, although they do not reproduce mechanically, a suggestive article by Jacob Bernard Agus, "The Covenant Concept—Particularistic, Pluralistic, or Futuristic," *Journal of Ecumenical Studies* 18:2 (1981), pp. 217–30.

2. See Yalkut Shimoni, Vaetchanan 6, no. 835.

3. This often-repeated phrase can be found throughout Abraham Joshua Heschel's writings, but see *The Insecurity of Freedom: Essays on Human Existence* (New York: Schocken, 1972), p. 93.

4. Jacob Neusner, *Torah From Our Sages, Pirke Avot: A New American Translation and Explanation* (Chappaqua, N.Y.: Rossel Books, 1984), pp. 115–16.

5. See Shmuel Hugo Bergman, *The Quality of Faith: Essays on Judaism and Morality* (Jerusalem: World Zionist Organization, 1970), pp. 64–89; see also *Bemishol* [Hebrew] (Tel Aviv: Am Oved, 1975), pp. 114–30.

6. Heschel, *A Passion for Truth* (New York: Farrar, Straus and Giroux, 1973), pp. 137–38.

7. Ibid., p. 312.

8. Ibid., p. 313.

9. Ibid., p. 323.

10. Ibid., p. 264.

11. See Irving Greenberg, "Clouds of Smoke, Pillar of Fire: Judaism, Christianity, and Modernity After the Holocaust," in *Auschwitz: Beginning of a New Era? Reflections on the Holocaust*, ed. Eva Fleschner (New York: Ktav, 1977), pp. 50–52; see also "Religious Values After the Holocaust: A Jewish View," in *Jews and Christians After the Holocaust*, ed. Abraham J. Peck (Philadelphia: Fortress Press, 1982), pp. 63–86.

12. See Berachot 6a-7a; Sanhedrin 46a.

13. Heschel, *A Passion for Truth*, p. 317.

14. Gershon Scholem, *The Messianic Idea in Judaism and Other Essays on Jewish Spirituality* (New York: Schocken, 1971), p. 35; see the entire essay, "Toward an Understanding of the Messianic Idea in Judaism," pp. 1–36.

15. Yonah Frankel, "The Image of Rabbi Joshua ben Levi in the Stories of the Babylonian Talmud," in *Proceedings of the Sixth World Congress of Jewish Studies*, Vol. III, pp. 403–17.

16. Heschel, *A Passion for Truth*, p. 42.

17. Menahem Mendel of Kotzk, *Emet ve Emunah*, 3d. rev. ed. (Jerusalem: 1972), p. 25.

18. Avodah Zarah 3a.

19. Stages of belief between youth and maturity characterize the discussions by Gordon W. Allport, *The Individual and His Religion* (New York: Macmillan, 1962); Erich Fromm, *Psychoanalysis and Religion* (New York: Bantam, 1967); and, most recently, James W. Fowler, *Stages of Faith* (San Francisco, Harper and Row, 1981).

20. Fowler, *Stages of Faith*, p. 300.

21. Maurice Friedman, *The Hidden Human Image* (New York: Dell,

1974), p. 367; see the entire discussion he devotes to this idea on pp. 358–71.

22.   Seymour J. Cohen, ed. and trans., *Orchot Zaddikim: The Ways of the Righteous* (New York: Ktav, 1982), p. 106.

6

Covenant Theology

COVENANT THEOLOGY AND THE MODERN JEW

The previous chapters explored the meaning that "covenant" might have as Jews seek to evolve a contemporary understanding of Jewishness. In every case, as will be made even clearer in this chapter, the meaning grows out of the concrete, practical reality in which Jews live. The need to affirm personal meaning derives from the absurd experiences of modern life; the tensions within civil religion reflect the inadequacy of any one political paradigm; the ecumenical imperative flows from the pluralistic experience of contemporary society. These statements focus on human needs. Martin Buber, however, has intimated that human needs mirror a divine need as well. He agrees that "you need God more than anything." He continues, however, by noting that "God needs you—in the fullness of his eternity."[1] This chapter suggests that analyzing human needs, examining the human side of covenant, reveals the hidden nature of God. The divine need for humanity emerges from recognizing how the world enables covenant obedience. Personal worth, communal dynamics, and ecumenical dialogue do not depend merely upon good will and virtuous intent. They are also part of the fabric of reality, they are conditioned by the facts of human existence. Uncovering their naturalness reveals their grounding in the divine.

UNITY AND DIVERSITY IN COVENANT

Maurice Friedman, as noted in the previous chapter, recognizes that the Kotzker legitimated religious differences — controversies for the sake of heaven preserve community. Friedman also suggests that interpretations of covenant as a univocal concept misunderstand the biblical tradition. He denies that God's covenant is "the exclusive possession" of any historical community. Every age must "renew" a covenant with God "according to the cruel but real demands of that age."[2] Such an understanding of covenant combines the various ideas suggested in the preceding chapters.

For each individual, covenant represents an imperative to evolve an interpretation of the facticity of life. Jews will create that interpretation drawing upon the resources of their tradition; different Jews will employ those resources differently; non-Jews draw upon different resources and will display an equally diverse variety of world views. Friedman warns his readers, however, that they can be misled, that "world views" may prove an obstacle to human meeting.[3]

The same danger applies to communal obligations. Covenant within the context of institutional paradigms, given the flexible and dynamic nature of covenant obligation applied to communities, also implies diversity. Such diversity may make life difficult for religious leaders. Friedman, for example, cites the Kotzker's awareness of the sacrificial nature of leadership. To be a leader is to be the "sacred goat," whose compassion leads him to sacrifice his horns for the sake of suffering humanity.[4] In response to this threat, some leaders may reduce their openness, may sacrifice the plurality of social and religious forms for the sake of establishing a more stable political order. Such a technique, however, leads to self-deception. Instead of creating true community, leaders who insist upon uniformity of belief, action, or values fashion a false community; they worship an idol of their own making.

Not only leaders within a community but individuals reaching out beyond the limits of their own group may fall prey to the same temptation for a universal religion. This vision seeks a set of universal ideals, a common human religion, as the basis for their affirmation of others whom they meet. Such an approach, however, leads to an equally false sense of human encounter. Active compassion will not settle for the appearance of human sharing or for the substitution of an imagined "other" created in one's own image for the real "other" whom one meets. The religions that human beings create may well be false religions; their purported ideals may lead away from genuine interaction rather than create opportunities for it. Friedman calls upon modern women and men to find their own "touchstones" by which to decide the "prevailing direction of religion."[5] Heeding such a call may enable Jews to avoid the danger that lurks in an ecumenical invitation to share values and symbols.

THE METAPHORS OF COVENANTAL JUDAISM

An exclusively rationalistic investigation of covenantal religion risks losing sight of the deep attraction to idolatry and oversimplification within any religion. Traditional Jewish teachings coped with the three aspects of covenant — personal, social, and universal — and the possibilities of abuse in each of them. Discovering the natural functions within them limits the risk of abuse. The metaphors for personal, social, and universal covenant present in Judaism suggest an important response to the dangers of parochialism, self-centeredness, and self-deceit inherent in any religious tradition. An ancient Jewish tradition (Avot 1:2) provides such metaphors when it declares that the world depends upon three things: Torah, holy service, and works of loving kindness. In its context the statement was probably a general comment on the value of the three major leadership groups in Jewish life — the rabbis, the priests, and the pietists. In general, the statement suggests, each of these three groups is essential for Jewish existence. As Jewish tradition developed, however, the statement took on ontological significance. Elijah Gaon of Vilna expounds this text in the tradition of Jewish mysticism (it should be remembered that although he opposed Hasidism as a popular anti-intellectualism, he also embraced the mystical tradition). He announces that "humanity, through the performance of the commandments, creates heaven and earth." With this in mind, he suggests that the three elements mentioned correspond to three types of obligations: those to the self, those to the divine, and those towards other people. Fulfilling obligations towards others "establishes the earth"; performing those towards God "establishes the heavens"; and actualizing those towards the self establishes both.[6] Torah provides a world view, worship a civil religion, and deeds of loving kindness an ecumenical perspective.

TORAH: COVENANT AS INDIVIDUAL CONSCIOUSNESS

By suggesting that worship focuses on civil religion and establishes the heavens, that ethical universalism creates an ideal human community, and that both require the cultivation of a sensitive world view, this understanding of Jewish metaphors gives concrete meaning to the phrase "Study of Torah is worth everything else." It implies that the personal world view cultivated by Jewish study becomes the basis for the creation of a social order through civil religion and of an ethics of interhuman meeting through deeds of loving kindness.

Since Torah, according to the Gaon of Vilna, includes both worship and deeds of loving kindness, an investigation of covenant as a modern Jewish metaphor should begin with the meaning of personal covenant as the basis for any modern Jewish theology. Torah, the first element in a modern Judaism, provides the means by which individuals discover who they are and how they understand the world in which they live.

Martin Buber records an encounter between the Alter Rebbe, Rabbi Sheneur Zalman, imprisoned by Russian authorities because he had been maligned by anti-Hasidic leaders, and the jailer who watched over him. The jailer, a pious Christian, tested the rabbi by asking religious questions. One question concerned the story of Adam as told in Genesis. After Adam disobeys God's command, he hides in the garden, and God calls out "Adam, where are you?" The jailer suggested that an omniscient deity would not need to ask such a question. The rabbi began his reply by claiming that God addresses that very question to every person, at every moment, demanding to know where they have come in their efforts at self-development, where they have come in the reality of their lives. He then turned to the questioner directly and demanded, "Now that you have lived forty years, where are you in your life?" Buber notes that the jailer was stirred to hear his own age mentioned by the rabbi.[7] The first obligation of Torah as personal covenant entails confronting the facts of one's own life, of taking stock of the place where one stands.

Torah in this sense requires Jews to create their own view of themselves as individuals, a view based on the facts of their existence. No individual, however, interprets the world in isolation. Torah is not read alone. At the very least the meaning of the world's facticity arises in association with an imagined community of others. As Jews listen to Torah and its demands upon their lives, they hear the voice of the past, and returning to it, they integrate what they have learned with what they have inherited. The covenant of Torah is thus a challenge to interpret the facticity of life. Torah summons Jews to awareness, awakening them from an uncritical acceptance of life's facticity and demanding an interpretation of it. Such a demand assumes a capability for imposing meaning on a set of facts. The jailer in the story must be able to make sense of the question put to him by the Torah; the answer to the question "Where are you?" cannot be given merely by citing statistics. Facts alone do not create a system of meaning; facticity itself does not entail meaning. Such meaning can occur only within community.

Although personal covenant emphasizes private identity, it

assumes the existence of a community that gives meaning to private life. The reality of community, despite the evidence of his own experience, convinces Ibn Verga's hero to affirm his tradition. Community, in precisely the sense meant here, C. H. Cooley suggests, represents a way of thinking, a perspective on life rather than an independent entity in and of itself. He understands it as an imaginative projection, a "phase of life." On this understanding, community refers to an internal reality, to an inner set of others to whom an individual looks for guidance. Cooley asserts that "there is always a circle of persons, more or less extended, whom we really imagine, and who thus work upon our impulses and our conscience" and that this imaginative reality should be termed "community."[8] Perhaps the existence of true Jewish community depends upon the creation of such an imaginative circle of others. In that case the tradition might well provide a resource from which to draw those others who will compose community.

Jewish teaching understands this necessity for an imaginative presentation of Jewish identity. Personal covenant obligates Jews to construct a sense of self based upon their connection with the past, to affirm meaning in the face of disconfirming evidence. The promise offered, the expectation created by this covenant agreement, seems exemplified in Cooley's contention. Jews receive an imaginative community in return for their loyalty to Jewish tradition, a collection of "other voices" informing their decisions. Buber interprets the Torah as a call to each person to review the meaning behind the facticity of life. The ability to heed such a call depends upon the strength of the imaginative community with which one identifies. God's presence in the life of each individual may be understood as the source of such a community, as the assurance that fulfilling the obligations of personal covenant will create a rich, imaginative resource for the interpretation of facts. The metaphor of Torah, then, must be interpreted as a symbol of the human imagination, of the varied sources and resources out of which individuals evolve their sense of reality. Torah conceived of as metaphor roots both the reality of community life and the ability to interact with others in the individual's inner existence. The richness and freedom of that internal life determine how full and open the individual's civil and ecumenical interactions will be.

WORSHIP AND THE FORMATION OF COVENANT COMMUNITY

While the communal voice in the imagination offers individuals a means of constructing identity, the concrete community, often expressed through worship and rituals, directs the creation of social reality. Will Herberg notes that all religious observances are an "acting out" of beliefs. The particular actions that emphasize Jewish existence — laws and observances that separate Jews from non-Jews — have as their major concern evoking the community of daily experience and the ideal — and inclusive — community commanded by covenantal duty.[9]

While obedience to the obligations of personal covenant reward an individual with an imaginative sense of community, communal covenantal obligations require a more substantial commitment. On the one hand, they demand that individuals accept the consensus of society. On the other hand, they require society itself to recognize the interdependency of all its members and include minorities within the full scope of communal existence. Thus the development of modern Jewish community demands the creation of responsive institutions no less than a stimulation of the Jewish identity through the assertion of a consistent world view. Louis Wirth suggests that human groups may be characterized on the basis of two dynamic elements: interdependency and consensus. He calls the first "community" and the second "society." Nevertheless, most groups share characteristics of each and learn to live with the tensions between them. Every community demonstrates either a common "basis of existence" or a "collective consciousness." Many collectivities, Wirth notes, possess neither and thus cannot really be thought of as either societies or as communities. A viable Jewish community, accordingly, validates its legitimacy by creating those institutions and possibilities by which both interdependence and consensus become the basis for ongoing human living.[10]

The central obligation of communal covenant for the individual lies in acceptance of the will of the Jewish group. Thus the institutions of Jewish life establish commandments as a means of unifying disparate Jews. The details of these commandments, however, differ widely throughout the five Books of Moses. Even the image of Moses as lawgiver indicates an ambiguity. At times Moses acts like a priest and not only invests his brother Aaron with the high priesthood, but gives detailed instructions on priestly behavior. Exodus 24, for example, describes how Moses fulfills various priestly functions, reads the covenant to the people, and accepts their declaration to obey all that the Lord says. At other times Moses seems to be the chief of the prophets and demands a high ethical standard: only to fear God, conform to His ways, and to serve Him wholeheartedly (Deuteronomy 10:12). The variety of Jewish institutional forms can be traced back to Moses and the covenant associated with him.

Mosaic law, then, often gives an ambiguous answer to a social question; the resolution of that ambiguity depends upon the consensus of the community. Covenant details are hammered out during social interaction; they may arise through religious agreement rather than by absolute fiat. A famous interpretation of Deuteronomy 30:12 (the Torah is not in heaven) insists that only scholarly consensus can determine a religious ruling.[11] Covenant implies communal agreement no less than communal interdependence in preserving the general welfare. As a document, the covenant creates a sense of identity and obligates those sharing that document to establish institutions for executing their obligations and for reaching a consensus on the practical details of those obligations. Minorities may often need to accept a compromise for the sake of consensus; institutions must yield to minority concerns out of recognition of interdependence. No one institutional stance can respond adequately to both demands. Thus covenantal awareness of the insufficiency of any single institutional paradigm receives its confirmation. Jewish tradition itself insists that no single model of covenant be absolutized, that no particular political form become the unalterable model for human community. While this dialectical theory appears simple in theory, applying it to Jewish life often proves difficult. Its very possibility evokes a recognition that the will of God cannot be easily discovered. The divine inheres in a dynamic process of community formation, not in any finalized actual community. Community itself, then, is a metaphor. Worship symbolizes a symbol! By creating a civil religion a community projects outward its inner sense of self. The community cannot be taken as an end in itself or as an independent entity. Its existence lies not "out there" in some objective sphere, but rather inheres in the consciousness of its members. Learning to take worship as a metaphor for community seriously, Jews recognize the evanescent reality of any particular form of communal leadership or authority.

THE UNIVERSAL MEANING OF JEWISH COVENANT

The institutions of Jewish life, despite their balance of consensus and interdependency, remain parochial in orientation. They focus on the needs of Jews and structures necessary for the preservation of Jewish community. Such an orientation may often lead to sterility and an unproductive isolation. Only when communal self-awareness points beyond itself to a general concern for all humanity does it animate true human living. Such a sense of humanistic purpose transforms the meaning of social life. A self-centered orientation evolves into a concentration on the general human meaning that should be the content of any social institution. Many writers have emphasized the need to infuse the structures of social life with an intimate content. While human community depends upon institutional limits for its existence, it requires free human interaction for its meaning. In this spirit of distinguishing between types of human collectivities, Victor Turner writes about "communitas" as a type of "anti-structure" necessary for the survival of group identity. He offers a typology for "communitas" itself — existential, normative, routinized — and links it to the type of direct, nonrational relationships described by Martin Buber. Turner's development of this aspect of community deserves comment as a particularly fruitful exploration of an important element in communal life.[12]

The implications of covenant as a paradigm for Jewish interaction with others suggests that obedience to covenant also creates communitas. The Hebrew Scriptures imply that one central purpose of covenantal law lies in sanctifying the people observing it. By animating parochial observances with humanistic meaning, an inclusive covenant fills institutions with significance. Exodus 33–34 explicitly sees the covenant code as a means by which an ordinary nation can withstand the holiness of the God accompanying them, a divine force that would to all expectations consume them with its power. Leviticus 19 propounds an even more extraordinary idea. The purpose of covenant laws lies in making those who follow them "holy as God is holy." That theme of sacralizing covenant members develops in later Judaism into the command to imitate the divine; Jews are to become the living image of divinity. The metaphor for loving kindness becomes that of imitating the love of the deity.

What does imitating the divine imply? A common answer — derived from Exodus 33–34 and expounded by authors such as Moses Maimonides in his *Moreh Nevuchim* — suggests that humanity must emulate God's loving, generous, and caring attributes. As God has demonstrated a willingness to enter into dialogue with human beings, so human beings must enter into dialogue with one another. This suggestion that the final meaning of covenant lies in its ethical implications finds confirmation by examining the content of the covenant idea itself in Jewish thought.

Covenant law regulates more than sacred memory or the relationship among social institutions. It also concerns both right belief, the intellectual sphere, and right action, ethics: the interaction among human beings. Such a law creates a community of ideas and a community of concerns. Covenant community, on that account, points to a group sharing a set of commitments and goals. Thus the reality of a covenant community may well be described as a framework within which true intimacy or communitas might take place.

Within Jewish tradition this final aspect of covenant has become known as "going beyond the strict limits of the law" (*lifnim mishurat hadin*).[13] Actions included under this rubric involve responsive concern for others. Although the letter of the law may allow employers to penalize incompetent workers, the demands of communitas prevent them from actualizing this permission.[14] Theologically, such actions represent an imitation of God. As God acts mercifully, so should human beings. The first five books of the Bible are bracketed by deeds of divine mercy. God clothes Adam and Eve; God buries Moses. Thus covenant, understood here as an obligation to transform the text of the Bible into living action, suggests that Jewish community depends as much upon spontaneous, loving responsiveness as upon its institutions or imaginative ideal.[15] Jewish ethics understands itself in a humanistic and open way. Covenant religion expects Jews to live in a community that evokes unmediated human relationships no less than those explicitly created by legal forms. Covenant responsibility entails a living human dialogue as the spiritual content of the institutions and of the social identity of Jewish life.

COVENANT IN MODERN JEWISH LIFE

Covenantal living depends upon fidelity to the obligations falling on each individual, on communal institutions, and on the community in its relationship to other communities. In each of these cases covenantal promises claim that the world supports and strengthens efforts to fulfill those obligations. Affirmation of a historic identity enables individuals to confront the facticity of life more adequately; maintaining flexibility of institutional paradigms preserves the flexibility of social responsiveness while retaining a necessary order and structure; creating an inclusive model for human interaction encourages that communitas upon which social life depends. Each element within the complex of covenantal theology justifies itself and its reinterpretive power for modern Judaism.

Covenant as a means of stimulating human betterment acts on every sphere of individual and social life. One great temptation in modern life is to think in global terms, to exalt great universal causes. In such cases people labor after herculean tasks while duties at home lie forgotten. The Hasidic teacher who learned progressively not to focus on the world, nor yet the town, nor yet his synagogue, nor even only on his family, but finally only on his own obligations, should provide a model of priorities. Covenantal obligations begin with the self, grow to communal awareness, and finally accept universal duties.

COVENANT AS A PRACTICAL CONCEPT

Covenant — whether taken as a model of individual selfhood, of communal duty, or of orientation towards others — presents a practical program of human living. The threefold approach found in that concept may well be emulated by modern Jews. Spiritual hope entails a religious activism — one must cultivate the needs of the soul. A social responsiveness to the needs of community as expressed by a balance between consensus and interdependence, however, must be taken seriously. Finally, such communal sensitivity should point beyond itself to interaction with those who are outside of the community.

Peter Berger contends that the great challenge before religion is theodicy — the defense of God. For modern Jews the more accurate description suggests the need for anthropodicy, a defense of humanity. Berger's schema, however, suggesting a scale of theodicy from "rationality to irrationality," proves useful in comprehending the volitional element in covenantal living.[16] Covenantal theology as presented here adequately measures up to the challenges of secularism.

Such a theology recognizes the presence of God in natural human experiences — in a social construction of reality, in communal institutional life, and in social experience. The transformation of traditional language about covenant into naturalistic language may seem to reduce the religious content it possesses. Can the retention of words such as "covenant" or "God" be justified in a naturalistic theology? The choice of language with which to describe reality represents a theological decision. This study emphasizes traditional language, even if that language is converted into naturalistic terms. Theology shapes the way believers perceive reality no less than that belief reflects the persuasiveness of the theological constructs. Using traditional language to express a non-traditional idea becomes a testimony to the power of conditioning. Such an approach admits that the means by which concepts are conveyed suggest more than the concept itself.

Peter Berger, exploring "the rediscovery of the supernatural," suggests that people today who search for the truth must do so by confronting their traditions in an ecumenical setting. He claims that the modern period creates an ecumenical consciousness that "makes possible a mode of theologizing that is very aware of the fullness of man's religious quest."[17] The presentation of the idea of covenant here seeks to realize Berger's claim and demonstrate a type of theologizing that not only helps Jews cope with modernity but that can also reveal to all readers the possibilities of human spirituality.

NOTES

1.   Martin Buber, *I and Thou,* a new translation with a prologue and notes by Walter Kaufmann (New York: Charles Scribner's Sons, 1970), p. 130.

2.   Maurice Friedman, *The Human Way: A Dialogic Approach to Religion and Human Experience* (Chambersburg, Pa.: Anima Books, 1982), p. 24.

3.   Ibid., p. 10.

4.   Ibid., p. 150.

5.   Ibid., pp. 187–89.

6.   See Tzvi Yehudah Gottlieb, ed., *Perkei Avot Im Perush Etz Ha-Sadeh* (Benei Barak: Ben David, 1984), pp. 6–7.

7.   See Buber, *Hasidism and Modern Man,* ed. and trans. Maurice Friedman (New York: Horizon Press, 1958), pp. 130–36.

8.   C. H. Cooley, *Human Nature and the Social Order,* introduction by Philip Rieff; foreword by George Herbert Mead (New York: Schocken, 1964), p. 390.

9.   Will Herberg, *Judaism and Modern Man: An Interpretation of Jewish Religion* (New York: Harper and Row, 1951), pp. 297–303.

10.   See Louis Wirth, *On Cities and Social Life: Selected Papers,* ed. Albert J. Reiss, Jr. (Chicago: University of Chicago Press, 1964).

11.   Baba Metziah 59b.

12.   See Victor Turner, *Dramas, Fields and Metaphors: Symbolic Action in Human Society* (Ithaca: Cornell University Press, 1974).

13.   See Saul Berman, "Lifnim Mishurat Hadin," *Journal of Jewish Studies* 26 (1975), pp. 86–104; 28 (1977), pp. 59–73.

14.   See Baba Metziah 83a.

15.   See David S. Shapiro, "The Concept of 'Chesed' in Judaism," in his *Studies in Jewish Thought* 1 (New York: Yeshiva University Press, 1975), pp. 98–121.

16.   Peter L. Berger, *The Sacred Canopy: Elements of a Sociological Theory of Religion* (Garden City, New York: Doubleday, 1969), pp. 53–80.

17.   Berger, *A Rumor of Angels: Modern Society and the Rediscovery of the Supernatural* (Garden City, New York: Doubleday, 1969), p. 80; see the discussion throughout the book.

Annotated Bibliography

While the majority of the works cited here also appear in the text and footnotes of this study proper, some additional works have been included because of their relevance to the covenant concept. Each entry includes a brief description summarizing the major contribution of the essay or book for a modern understanding of Jewish covenant. Some of the thinkers most important in the body of this study — for example, Maurice Friedman, from whom I have learned incalculably — do not appear in this annotated bibliography because their work ranges more generally than the theory of covenant. This bibliography should not replace the analysis given in the main text but serve to stimulate further research on the part of readers.

Agus, Jacob Bernard. "The Covenant Concept — Particularistic, Pluralistic, or Futuristic." *Journal of Ecumenical Studies* 18 (1982), pp. 217–30.
　　Agus reviews Jewish thinking on the idea of covenant from the biblical, medieval, and modern periods. He concludes that covenant may imply different concepts. He prefers the idea of covenant as an image of the future.

Bergman, Samuel Hugo. "The Humanism of the Covenant." In *The Quality of Faith: Essays on Judaism and Morality*, trans. Yehudah Hanegbi, pp. 64–89. Jerusalem: World Zionist Organization, 1970.
　　Bergman emphasizes that Judaism is a religion of community and covenant rather than the solitary individual; it represents a vision of messianic community, not of individual redemption.

Borowitz, Eugene B. "The Jewish People Concept as it Affects Jewish Life in the Diaspora." *Journal of Ecumenical Studies* 12 (1975), pp. 553–86.
　　Borowitz offers a cogent reinterpretation of the Jewish view of covenant and chosenness for modern Jews uncomfortable with the idea

of covenant as a one-sided divine fiat. His reasoned presentation suggests the seriousness of the covenant idea for modern Jewish theologians.

Bruce, F. F. "The Theology and Interpretation of the Old Testament." In *Tradition and Interpretation: Essays by Members of the Society for the Study of the Old Testament*, ed. G. W. Anderson, pp. 385–416. Oxford: Clarendon Press, 1979.
Bruce surveys Christian theologies of the Hebrew Scriptures and notes that those emphasizing covenant sometimes misunderstand the diversity of covenantal options in the texts.

Buber, Martin. "The Election of Israel: A Biblical Inquiry." In *On the Bible*, ed. Nahum N. Glatzer, pp. 80–92. New York: Schocken, 1968.
Buber's studies in general illuminate covenant as a modern Jewish category of religious thinking. This essay focuses on the idea of chosenness and its essential meaning as a category of covenant and should be compared to his other works.

Cohen, Martin. "The Mission of Israel After Auschwitz." In *Issues in the Jewish-Christian Dialogue: Jewish Perspectives on Covenant, Mission, and Witness*, eds. Helga Croner and Leon Klenicki, pp. 157–80. New York: Paulist Press, 1979.
Cohen's study moves from biblical paradigms to conclusions about covenant and its obligation for modern Jews. He insists that Jewish witness suggests that covenantal thinking should characterize not only Jewish culture but that of western civilization generally.

Eisen, Arnold M. *The Chosen People in America: A Study of Jewish Religious Ideology*. Bloomington: Indiana University Press, 1983.
Eisen's careful study demonstrates the way American Jews wrestle with the idea of covenant, focusing on the thinking of such philosophers as Mordecai Kaplan, Eugene Borowitz, and Emil Fackenheim. Eisen concludes that nontraditional Jews find an affirmation of covenantal chosenness nearly impossible and fail to adequately grasp the significance of the holocaust.

Fackenheim, Emil L. *To Mend the World: Foundations of Future Jewish Thought*. New York: Schocken, 1982.
Fackenheim's thinking represents a major interpretation of covenant for contemporary Jews. This book focuses on the Jewish task after the holocaust and in a world that includes a reborn Jewish state.

Fackenheim, Emil L. *God's Presence in History: Jewish Affirmations and Philosophical Reflections*. New York: Harper and Row, 1970.
This short interpretation of Jewish covenantal thinking based on the story of the Exodus from Egypt suggests ways of understanding modern Jewish history — especially the holocaust and the modern State of Israel — within a covenantal paradigm.

Goldberg, Michael. *Jews and Christians: Getting Our Stories Straight: The Exodus and the Passion-Resurrection*. Nashville: Abingdon, 1985.
Goldberg's careful reading of the "Jewish Master Story" in Exodus offers a convincing interpretation of covenantal symbolism. His emphasis upon story as the basis of religious thinking illustrates a major aspect of covenant theology.

Hartman, David. *A Living Covenant: The Innovative Spirit in Traditional Judaism*. New York: The Free Press, 1985.
This refreshing, creative, and daring work prepares the foundation for an innovative traditional Judaism. Hartman surveys the major thinkers and issues dominating contemporary traditional Jewish theology and steers a distinctive course between the various options. While concerned with general ideas and basic principles, Hartman's discussion of covenant offers a valuable glimpse of a flexible traditional Judaism.

Heinemann, Isaac. "The Election of Israel." [Hebrew], *Sinai* 8 (1944/45), pp. 17–30.
Heinemann studies the basic primary sources out of which Jews evolve their sense of election and covenantal duties. He notes both the scandal of chosenness and the restraint that diaspora life places on Jewish covenantal thinking.

Herberg, Will. *Faith Enacted as History: Essays in Biblical Theology*, edited with an introduction by Bernhard W. Anderson. Philadelphia: Westminster, 1976.
The various essays in this work illustrate how one modern Jewish theologian interprets the covenant story and its meaning. Herberg's insistence on the centrality of the Exodus story and his use of it to explain the totality of Jewish living represent an important modern Jewish statement of covenantal responsibility.

Heschel, Abraham Joshua. *The Insecurity of Freedom: Essays on Human Existence*. New York: Schocken, 1972.

Heschel's philosophy of Judaism takes covenantal theology as a point of departure, as his various books on theology show. This particular collection of essays illustrates how he employs biblical categories to confront contemporary Jewish issues.

Katz, Steven T. "Covenant" and "Chosen People." In *Jewish Ideas and Concepts*, pp. 156–62, pp. 163–69. New York: Schocken, 1977.
These clear presentations sketch the development of the covenant idea and the chosen people idea in its historical context. They are particularly valuable as introductions to the theological concepts as part of the history of Jewish thought.

Kirschenbaum, Aaron. "The Noahide Covenant as Contrasted With the Covenant at Sinai." *Dine Israel* 6 (1975), pp. 31–48.
This clear exposition of Jewish views of covenant demonstrates that covenant may imply different obligations for different covenant communities. That Jews and non-Jews each have covenant relationships with God does not imply their equivalence.

Levenson, Jon. D. "Covenant and Commandment." *Tradition* 21 (1983), pp. 42–51.
This careful study distinguishes between two types of covenant in the Hebrew Bible. As such it demonstrates the tension within the covenantal concept and its ambivalence within Jewish religion.

Mann, Thomas Wingate. *Divine Presence and Guidance in Israelite Traditions: The Typology of Exaltation*. Baltimore: Johns Hopkins University Press, 1977.
This study of biblical religion reviews the work of major scholars, including the studies by Martin Buber, and concludes that the covenant idea, as understood throughout the ancient Near East, provides a basic biblical paradigm.

McCarthy, Dennis J. *Old Testament Covenant: A Survey of Current Opinions*. Growing Points in Theology. Richmond: John Knox, 1972.
McCarthy offers a review of biblical scholarship and its study of the covenant formula in the ancient Near East. He provides examples of extra-biblical covenantal forms and summarizes the diverse interpretations given by biblical critics.

Nicholson, Ernest W. *God and His People: Covenant and Theology in the Old Testament*. Oxford: Clarendon Press, 1986.

Nicholson summarizes biblical scholarship as it gradually accepted the covenantal idea as an ancient one. He traces the idea of covenant through various parts of the Bible and demonstrates how ancient Israel adapted and transformed the concept. Nicholson's careful delineation of particular biblical texts informs this book with a wealth of detail and precision.

Novak, David. "The Logic of the Covenant: An Essay in Systematic Jewish Theology." In *Halakhah in a Theological Dimension*, pp. 116–31. Chico, California: Scholar's Press, 1985.

Novak draws on classical and medieval Jewish sources to offer an interpretation of the multivalence of the concept of covenant. He shows the dialectic between activity and passivity in Jewish understanding of covenantal obligation and in the revelation from which it derives.

Plaut, W. Gunther. *The Case for the Chosen People*. New York: Doubleday, 1965.

Plaut confronts the basic challenges to Jewish self-understanding as a chosen people. He discovers in covenantal dialectic that Jews are both choosing and chosen and that the significance of Jewish covenantal life should be understood as obligation and duty.

Polish, David. "Covenant — Jewish Universalism and Particularism." *Judaism* 34:3 (1985), pp. 284–300.

Polish analyzes basic biblical and post-biblical texts concerning covenant — circumcision, the Prophets, Noah, and the various covenant-making and covenant-renewal ceremonies, including the story told by Ibn Verga in the Shevet Yehuda. He concludes that the covenantal idea includes both universal and particularistic meaning and that Jews and non-Jews are bound together in responsibility.

Rubenstein, Richard L. "Religion and History: Power, History and the Covenant at Sinai." In *Take Judaism, for Example: Studies Toward the Comparison of Religions*, ed. Jacob Neusner, pp. 165–183. Chicago: University of Chicago Press, 1983.

All of Rubenstein's writings show a sensitivity to the ambiguity of Jewish theology. This essay looks particularly at the idea of covenant and demonstrates its ability to reinforce conservative as well as liberal politics. The article reveals his ability to recognize how modernity creates a new Jewish sensibility.

Schachter, Lifsa. "Reflections on the Brit Mila Ceremony." *Conservative Judaism* 38:4 (1986), pp. 38–41.
Schachter analyzes what is perhaps the quintessential covenant ceremony in Jewish life. He discovers that its associations suggest the breadth of meaning Judaism gives to that concept.

Schechter, Solomon. "The Election of Israel." In *Aspects of Rabbinic Theology*, pp. 57–64. New York: Schocken, 1961.
Schechter's classic discussion of Israel's election suggests the biblical and Talmudic basis for the idea. He recognizes the variety of Jewish interpretations and insists upon the universalism implicit in the idea.

Schwarzschild, Steven S. "On the Theology of Jewish Survival." In *Judaism and Ethics*, ed. Daniel Jeremy Silver, pp. 287–314. New York: Ktav, 1976.
Schwarzschild insists that covenant existence is for God's sake. While he finds that this essay has often been quoted out of context, his contention that covenantal theology opposes Israeli triumphalism represents the view of many contemporary Jews, as does his understanding of the relationship between covenant obligation and Jewish intermarriage.

Spriggs, D. G. "Eichrodt's Theology of Covenant." In *Two Old Testament Theologies*, pp. 11–33. SBT 2d series, 30. Naperville: Alec R. Allenson, 1974.
Spriggs offers a summary and critique of one of the major biblical theologians who uses covenant as a basic category.

Trible, Phyllis. *God and the Rhetoric of Sexuality*. Philadelphia: Fortress, 1978.
Trible's writings express the searching of many contemporary feminists and their analysis of biblical writings. She demonstrates how the place of women in the covenant community tests the authenticity of the religious impulse it expresses.

Wyschogrod, Michael. *The Body of Faith: Judaism as Corporeal Election*. New York: Seabury Press, 1983.
Wyschogrod defends traditional Judaism with a vigorous and persuasive argument. His affirmation of covenant and Jewish chosenness reflects a modern Jewish orthodoxy that recognizes its authenticity and its message to the non-Jewish world.

Zimmerli, W. "The History of Israelite Religion." In *Tradition and Interpretation: Essays By Members of the Society for Old Testament Studies*, ed. G. W. Anderson, pp. 351–84. Oxford: Clarendon Press, 1979.

Zimmerli recognizes the variety of covenantal types within the biblical tradition. As a biblical scholar, he accurately reflects the diversity of covenant within the Bible.

Index

ABOUT THE AUTHOR

S. DANIEL BRESLAUER is Associate Professor of Religious
Studies at the University of Kansas. He is the author of several
books and articles, including *Modern Jewish Morality: A Bibliographical Survey* (Greenwood, 1986) and *Contemporary
Jewish Ethics: A Bibliographical Survey* (Greenwood, 1985).

DATE DUE

HIGHSMITH #LO-45220